The Nine Old Men

Learn from the men who changed animation forever.

Walt Disney's team of core animators, who he affectionately called his "Nine Old Men," were known for creating Disney's most famous works, as well as refining the 12 basic principles of animation. Follow master animator and Disney legend Andreas Deja as he takes you through the minds and works of these notable animators. An apprentice to the Nine Old Men himself, Deja gives special attention to each animator and provides a thoughtful analysis of their techniques, which include figure drawing, acting, story structure, and execution. The in-depth analysis of each animator's work will allow you to refine your approach to character animation. Rare sequential drawings from the Walt Disney Animation Research Library also give you unprecedented access and insight into the most creative minds that changed the course of animation.

- Instruction and analysis on the works of each of the Nine Old Men broaden your creative choices and approaches to character animation.
- Original drawings, some never-before-seen by the public, are explored in depth, giving you behind-the-scenes access into Disney animation history.
- Gain first-hand insight into the foundation of timeless characters and scenes from some of Disney's most memorable feature and short films.

Andreas Deja was ten years old when he first applied for a job as a Disney animator. The studio wrote back to Deja telling him that they had no openings, but were always on the lookout for new talent. At the age of 20, he applied again and was accepted. This launched a long and successful career with Disney. Deja has left his mark on some of the most memorable and successful Disney animated features and shorts. His early work includes animation and character design for *The Great Mouse Detective*, *Oliver & Company*, and *Who Framed Roger Rabbit*. In addition, he is known for his animation of some of Disney's most evil villains: Gaston, Jafar, and Scar. The list of memorable characters continues with King Triton, Mickey Mouse, Hercules, Lilo, Goofy, Tigger, Mama Odie, and Juju. In 2006, at the 35th Annie Awards, Deja was awarded the Winsor McCay Award for outstanding contribution to the art of animation. In 2015, he was named a Disney Legend by the Walt Disney Company. Presently, Deja is working on his own independent animated short films and is actively involved in his animation-related blog, *Deja View*.

The Nine

LESSONS, TECHNIQUES, AND INSPIRATION
FROM DISNEY'S GREAT ANIMATORS

Andreas Deja

Old Men

CRC Press
Taylor & Francis Group

A FOCAL PRESS BOOK

CRC Press
Taylor & Francis Group
6000 Broken Sound Parkway NW, Suite 300
Boca Raton, FL 33487-2742

© 2016 Taylor & Francis

CRC Press is an imprint of the Taylor & Francis Group, an informa business

Library of Congress Cataloging in Publication Data
Deja, Andreas, 1957–
The nine old men : lessons, techniques, and inspiration from Disney's great animators / Andreas Deja.
    pages cm
1. Animation (Cinematography)—Miscellanea. 2. Animators—United States. 3. Animated films—United States—History—20th century. 4. Walt Disney Productions—History—20th century. I. Title.
    TR897.5.D45 2015
    777'.7—dc23
    2015010907

ISBN: 978-0-415-84335-5 (hbk)
ISBN: 978-0-203-75661-4 (ebk)

Designed and typeset by Alex Lazarou
(alexlazarou@aol.com)

Visit the Taylor & Francis Web site at http://www.taylorandfrancis.com
and the CRC Press Web site at http://www.crcpress.com

I dedicate this book to Eric Larson, who saw my potential as an animator
when I was still an art student, and eventually hired me to join
Walt Disney Productions' Animation Department.

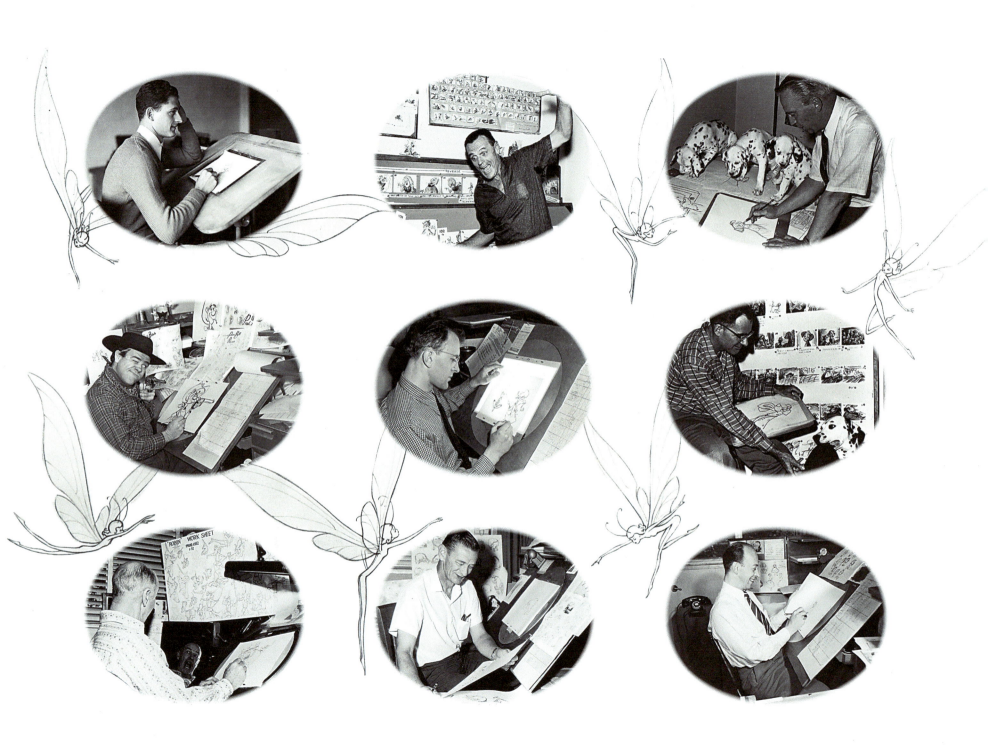

CONTENTS

ACKNOWLEDGMENTS

I express my deep gratitude to everybody, who shared my enthusiasm for this book project from day one. They are:

- My editors from Focal Press. Lauren Mattos, who asked me in the first place whether I was interested in sharing my knowledge in the art of Disney's Nine Old Men, and Caitlin Murphy, who patiently oversaw the bulk of this book's production. Both Lauren and Caitlin gave me the kind of warm guidance that was very much appreciated by this first time-writer.
- Members of Disney's fabulous Animation Research Library (ARL). Mary Walsh, the managing director, who supported the project by delegating a number of knowledgeable staff members to help research endless visual materials.
- Research manager Fox Carney patiently stood by me during my long selection process and provided me with numerous scans of beautiful artwork I didn't even know still existed.
- Researchers Jackie Vasquez, Ann Hansen, and Doug Engella, all searched methodically for animation drawings that best complemented my writings.
- Eric Boyd conducted some tasteful clean-up and prepping of the files.
- Michael Pucher, Mathieu Fretschel, and Idris Erba from the Image Capture Team photographed some art from my personal collection of animation art.
- Last not least Roger Viloria, who helped me to select and scan original drawings I had accumulated over the years.

During the whole process of writing and gathering gorgeous material for this book I found myself in a state of utter delight and kept thinking that there really is no better time spent than researching the masterworks of Walt Disney's incomparable animators.

Photo by Roger Viloria

Andreas Deja first applied for a job as a Disney animator at the age of ten. Born in Poland and raised in Germany, he remembers writing to the studio immediately after seeing *The Jungle Book*. "I'd never seen a Disney feature before," he recalls. "It was one of those key experiences because I just couldn't believe what I'd seen. All those drawings moving, thinking, and acting so real."

The studio wrote back to Deja explaining that there were no openings but they were always on the lookout for new talent. This offered him the encouragement he needed and the motivation to work hard towards that goal. At the age of 20, after completing his studies, he applied again and this time he was accepted.

Working with Eric Larson, one of Disney's legendary "Nine Old Men," Deja completed several tests and went on to do early character design, costume research, and animation for *The Black Cauldron* (1985). His next assignment was on *The Great Mouse Detective* (1986), for which he animated the mouse queen and her robotic twin. Deja helped design many of the characters for *Oliver & Company* (1988) and did some animation before spending a year in London as a lead animator on *Who Framed Roger Rabbit* (1988), under the direction of Richard Williams.

On *The Little Mermaid* (1989), Deja oversaw the animation of King Triton, a powerful figure that required expert skills in draftsmanship and acting ability. For Disney's Academy Award-winning animated musical *Beauty and the Beast* (1991), he served as the supervising animator for the first of his many Disney villains, the very pompous and narrow-minded Gaston.

Deja continued to explore his darker side by designing and animating the evil vizier Jafar for Disney's animated musical hit *Aladdin* (1992). He went on to supervise the animation of the power-hungry villain, Scar, in *The Lion King* (1994), which quickly earned a place as one of the industry's biggest films of all time.

For his next assignment, Deja relocated to Disney's Paris animation facility for a stint overseeing the animation of Mickey Mouse in *Runaway Brain*, the studio's first new Mickey short since 1953 and an Oscar nominee in 1996 for Best Animated Short. Following that, he returned to Burbank, where he took on the challenging assignment of bringing life and personality to the title hero in Disney's 35th full-length animated feature, *Hercules* (1997). He went on to design and supervise the animation for the charming and unpredictable little Hawaiian girl Lilo in *Lilo & Stitch* (2002), which has been hailed as one of the studio's most entertaining and imaginative features.

Deja contributed animation for several characters in Disney's live-action/animated musical *Enchanted* (2007), and served as one of the supervising animators on Goofy's big-screen return in the short film, *How to Hook Up Your Home Theater* (2007). He was a supervising animator on Disney's hand-drawn animated feature *The Princess and the Frog*, released in 2009. He also supervised the animation of Tigger for a new Winnie the Pooh feature, which was released theatrically in 2011.

In 2007, he was honored with the Winsor McKay Award from ASIFA (the International Animated Film Association).

Currently, Andreas Deja is working on his own independent animated short films. He also contributes regularly animation-related material on his blog *Deja View*.

PREFACE

*O*ne day in the late 1970s I discussed Disney animation with my life-drawing teacher. "Anybody can learn how to animate like Disney," he claimed. "It's all technique, but no art." I was shocked! This man was a terrific teacher and an artist in his own right. I doubted his judgment quietly, having already spent endless hours studying the fluid motion of Disney animation with the help of Super-8 film clips. I could not imagine that anybody could learn to animate like this by picking up a few simple tricks. It seemed to me that in order to create life through drawings, an artist had to become very involved and committed.

My art school didn't offer any animation classes, which meant if I wanted to pursue a future career in animation, a self-taught method would be the only option. After giving myself assignments like walk cycles and other pencil tests, I found out that Disney Studios had started a training program for new talent joining the animation department. It turned out that veteran animator Eric Larson worked with newcomers on developing their craft to eventually become fully fledged animators.

About one year later, in August 1980, I applied for the program and was lucky enough to get accepted. One of the things I remember is Eric going over my drawings from a scene I was trying to animate. Looking over the shoulder of one of Disney's great animators and watching him as he strengthened my poses and timing was intimidating and thrilling at the same time.

When viewing my corrected scene, I couldn't believe my eyes. Eric's input added pure magic; the character's actions became more clear and believable. What started out as messy graphic motion, now seemed to show signs of life.

It was Eric who first introduced me to two other Disney animators, Frank Thomas and Ollie Johnston, who were in the midst of writing their first book on Disney animation, *The Illusion of Life*. Conversations with these artists were fascinating because, after all, they had been involved with almost all of Disney's animated films. These movies shaped my childhood and made me wonder, how on earth this level of excellence was achieved. Now I had the opportunity to ask endless questions about the art of character animation.

When I was still in Germany, the term "Disney's Nine Old Men" had been familiar to me; I knew the names of this elite group of animators from books and magazine articles.

What I wasn't aware of was the fact that two of them had already passed away when I started working for the studio. John Lounsbery and Les Clark were no longer alive, but I was lucky to get to know and become friends with seven of the nine, including Eric Larson, Frank Thomas, and Ollie Johnston.

Woolie Reitherman still worked at the studio during the early 1980s, developing ideas for new projects. Marc Davis had retired, but lived close by, and he and his wife Alice enjoyed interacting with a new generation of animators. Ward Kimball lectured occasionally at the studio and was always up for a lunch date. Milt Kahl had moved to San Francisco after spending more than 40 years as an animator at Disney. I visited him once or twice a year and, despite his rough reputation, found him to be generous with his time and stimulating to talk to. I was lucky to be able to join Disney at a time when so many master animators were still alive and, as it turned out, very approachable. Every conversation with each of them left me incredibly inspired and compelled to study their work in greater detail. At that time the studio kept all of the animated, hand-drawn scenes ever done in a makeshift archive called the Morgue, which was placed in the basement of the Ink and Paint Department. Newcomers like myself were encouraged to study this material up close and learn from it. And what a school it was! Whether it was Medusa pulling off her false eyelashes, Bambi chasing a butterfly, or Baloo dancing with Mowgli, flipping those scenes left me with a feeling of either frustration—I am never going to be as good as this—or utter elation—look how incredible this medium can be!

In this book I try to share anecdotes and reflections by these incredible artists—as related to me—and present some of their brilliant work.

My art teacher was wrong; Disney animation is so much more than technique. Creating personalities on the screen through drawings is extremely difficult and only succeeds if the animator finds a way to express him- or herself personally. As Marc Davis said, it is the ultimate art form, involving drawing, acting, music, dancing, and painting, all combined into one medium.

The Nine Old Men

Les Clark

*W**hen** Les Clark retired from the animation industry in 1975 he had worked for Walt Disney Productions for almost half a century. He first met Walt Disney in 1925 at the candy store he was working for part-time, as Clark was still attending high school. A couple of years later, with no formal art training but an avid interest in the new medium of animation, he asked Walt for a job.

His portfolio consisted only of a few redrawn illustrations from the popular magazine *College Humor*, but Disney saw something in his lively line work, and so Les was hired in 1927. He spent his first year at the studio as a camera operator. Clark also learned the craft of inking the animators' drawings on celluloid sheets, so-called cels, before they were photographed on a painted background under the camera. Eventually he became an in-betweener on scenes with Oswald the Lucky Rabbit. When Walt Disney found himself in a feud with his film distributor, who owned the character's rights, he refused to renew a less attractive contract and walked away from the Oswald film series. Walt was in need of a new character, and soon Mickey Mouse was born. Animator Ub Iwerks drew the first couple of Mickey shorts, *Plane Crazy* and *The Gallopin' Gaucho*, and his assistant Les Clark did the in-betweens. But it was Mickey's third film *Steamboat Willie* that resonated with audiences in a big way. Walt produced this short with sound, and the enthusiastic response was a big shot in the arm for the struggling animation studio. New Mickey films followed to great success, but Walt also wanted to diversify and started another series called Silly Symphonies, in which music played a vital role. The first one was *The Skeleton Dance*, which again was mostly animated by Iwerks. Clark got the chance to draw a scene in which one skeleton uses the ribcage of another one like a xylophone.

A couple of frivolous skeletons marked the beginning of Clark's career as an animator.
© Disney

In these early days of animation, many discoveries were about to be made, and squash and stretch was one of them. By distorting the character's face and overall body mass, the illusion of life suddenly became more believable than ever before. It seemed that by showing change within the rhythm of the character, the animated performances became much more convincing.

One character that came to life through extensive use of squash and stretch was Clara Cluck in the short *Orphan's Benefit*. She plays an eccentric opera singer during a talent show that is hosted by Mickey Mouse. Clark animated her entering the stage with a weighty walk. Her hefty body parts move with overlapping motion, and the effect is entertaining and convincing. As she sings her aria, Clark again uses dramatic distortions in her body to emphasize the high notes.

Clark used strong squash and stretch on the character of Clara Cluck in the short Orphan's Benefit. *© Disney*

3

Les Clark had absorbed all of Iwerks' work methods including his way of staging gags convincingly. Characters needed to be drawn in clear silhouette in order to communicate their humorous antics. There was also a surreal quality to those gags; nothing seemed impossible. When Minnie jumps out of an airplane to get away from Mickey, her panties turn into a parachute and she lands safely. Crude as this might seem today, animated gags like this got big laughs from audiences at the time. When Iwerks left Disney to open his own animation studio, Clark became the lead animator for Mickey Mouse.

In 1935, Mickey starred in his first color short film *The Band Concert*, in which he conducts an orchestra out in the open. After several interruptions by characters like Horace Horsecollar and Donald Duck, a tornado suddenly strikes. But Mickey keeps his cool and continues to direct his musicians, even when everybody is being lifted up high in the air by the storm. Les Clark animated all of the important scenes with Mickey, whose movements needed to be in sync with the music at all times. The animation is already smoother than what Iwerks had achieved with the character early on. But Disney's ongoing demands for improved animated performances would soon lead to breathtaking new heights in the art of character animation.

A young artist named Fred Moore had been assisting Clark's scenes, but during the early 1930s came into his own as an animator. He was a natural, intuitive draftsman, who never seemed to struggle with any of his assignments. Everything he drew had appeal and personality. To the envy of many of his colleagues, Walt Disney encouraged his animators to study Moore's style in order to capture some of its special charm. By 1936, Moore had redefined the design for Disney characters, and his way of drawing influenced the entire studio. One particular detail is worth pointing out; many of the early characters were given very simple eyes, usually a couple of vertical oval shapes, painted solid black. Moore created realistic eye units, in which oval white shapes were drawn with small black pupils. This resulted in a greater facial expressive range as well as subtle eye articulation. Animators Art Babbitt and Les Clark made full use of this new concept when they both animated Abner the mouse

Les Clark added greater appeal and range to Mickey's performances.
© Disney

4

Finish

TR. BAL #50

wm.
59

TRACE BAL #50

61
RT

Abner the country mouse with a mouthful of cheese.
© Disney

for the film *The Country Cousin*. Both artists also pushed the boundaries of elasticity when it came to exaggerate expressions. Clark animated a series of scenes in which the country mouse, looking at mountains of human food, can't help himself but stuff his mouth in the broadest way possible.

Broad as well as nuanced performances were needed to bring the group of dwarfs to life for Disney's first feature film *Snow White and the Seven Dwarfs*. Clark had the experience and the talent to animate important acting scenes. Fred Moore's cartoony designs of the dwarfs allowed for the kind of rich, fluid movements that most animators enjoyed. During the film's yodel song, Snow White enjoys the dwarfs' individual musical performances, before joining them for a dance.

Clark animated several scenes of the dwarfs playing different instruments including Sleepy, who plays a flute. At one point he pauses and gets into a big yawn, when suddenly a pesky housefly inspects the inside of Sleepy's wide-open mouth. The unwelcome visitor is quickly chased away with brisk hand-gestures. The scene is just over six seconds long, yet every bit of action reads very clearly. Enough time is given to each part of the performance: the yawn, the intruding insect, Sleepy's realization of what is happening, and him taking action.

Clark animated Sleepy playing a flute in Snow White and the Seven Dwarfs.
© *Disney*

It comes as no surprise that Les Clark got to animate many scenes with Pinocchio, the title character of Disney's second feature. While Milt Kahl, Frank Thomas and Ollie Johnston supervised Pinocchio's animation, Clark had no problems helping out wherever he was needed.

When, toward the end of the film, Geppetto is reunited with the wooden boy inside the whale's stomach, Clark gave some insightful performances. After a big sneeze, Pinocchio's donkey ears pop out from under his hat, shocking not only Geppetto, but Figaro the cat, and Cleo the goldfish. This is an awkward situation, and Pinocchio is at a loss for words. He holds his donkey tail, deeply embarrassed. The feeling of guilt and shame is beautifully portrayed in these poignant scenes. This is one of many Clark scenes that give us strong insight into how the character is feeling in a moment of embarrassment.

Sincere emotions help to make Pinocchio *come alive to an audience.*
© *Disney*

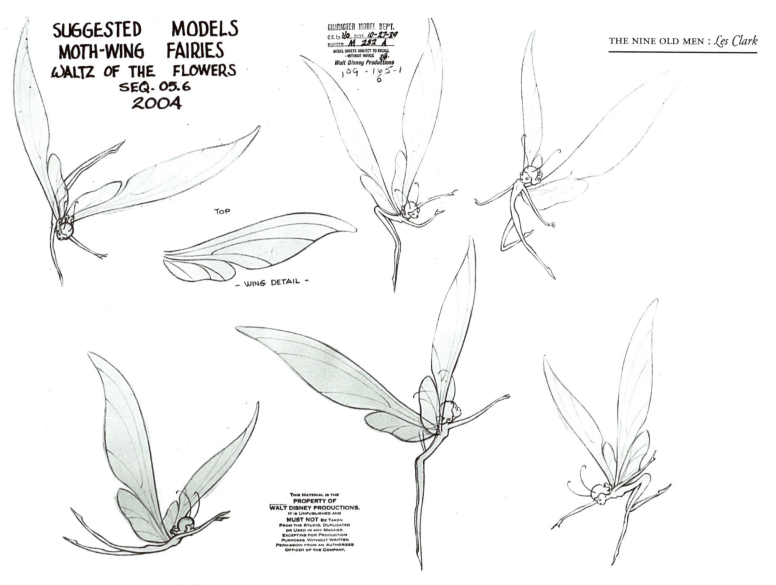

SUGGESTED MODELS
MOTH-WING FAIRIES
WALTZ OF THE FLOWERS
SEQ. 05.6
2004

CHARACTER MODEL DEP'T.
O.K. by ___ DATE 10-27-39
NUMBER M 252 A
MODEL SHEETS SUBJECT TO RECALL
· WITHOUT NOTICE
Walt Disney Productions
109 - 165 - 1
6

TOP

— WING DETAIL —

A very different type of assignment came along when Les Clark started to work on *Fantasia*: he animated a variety of fairies for the film's *Nutcracker Suite*. The development of specific personalities was not required, since we never get to know these nature sprites. Clark based their elegant movements on hummingbirds, which gave their flying patterns a beautiful stop-and-go feeling. These delicate fairies were drawn with sizable wings and long legs, which helped to define charming feminine poses.

Delicate drawing and subtle timing added a graceful touch to the fairies.
© Disney

7

Clark also animated an important part of *The Sorcerer's Apprentice*. When Mickey Mouse commands the broom to come to life, he does so with great intensity. While his body is stretched in a strong forward arch, his fingers flutter fiercely. This convulsion-like movement heightens the scene's tension and makes us believe that there are real magical powers at play. This is an extraordinary piece of animation, dramatically staged and perfectly timed. It also shows an intensity in Mickey's emotions that had not been seen before. His attitude changes after he succeeds in making the broom follow him to a fountain. Clark animates Mickey here with a confident attitude, as he hops along and leads the way. The movement is made interesting by the addition of complex overlapping action in Mickey's oversized coat. Realistic designs of the fabric's folds perfectly enhance the character's bouncy motion.

In The Sorcerer's Apprentice, *Clark gave Mickey an intensity that had not been seen before.*
© *Disney*

While Mickey might have been conducting the universe in *Fantasia*, in the 1942 short film *The Symphony Hour* he is in charge of an impaired orchestra, which consists of classic Disney characters like Donald Duck, Goofy and Horace Horsecollar. Mickey had gone through a few design changes during the early 1940s. The inside of his ears were painted in grey, and they almost moved dimensionally. In previous films his perfectly round ears just slid across his upper head. While his torso was drawn a bit smaller, more volume was given to his nose, hands, and feet. Les Clark animated the opening scenes when the musicians try very hard to follow Mickey's lead. As an animator it would be a challenge to find interesting ways for the conductor's movements, particularly when the beat is fairly even, as it is in this section of the film. But Clark varies Mickey's hand gestures just enough to give the animation texture. Each hand action needs to end one or two frames ahead of the actual sound in order to feel in sync with the music.

With The Symphony Hour, *Clark showed again that he was an expert at animating Mickey Mouse.*
© *Disney*

Music also played a role, when it came to bringing a little train to life during a short section from the film *The Three Caballeros*. José Carioca invites Donald Duck to join him on a train ride to the city of Baia. Les Clark's animation of the spirited locomotive is charming, as it chugs along to an energetic musical beat through a landscape that is reminiscent of a children's book illustration. The movements evoke the alluring simplicity found in the work of Clark's former mentor Ub Iwerks. All goes well on the journey until the naughty Aracuan Bird draws separating tracks on the ground, which causes the little train to lose all his wagons for a few tense moments, until they all get reunited near the train station. This train goes through real human emotions, from having fun to anxiety and then relief at the end of the sequence. No arms or legs needed, not even a face. Yet Clark articulates these feelings by offsetting the various locomotive parts in a way that communicates a definitive state of mind.

The train in The Three Caballeros *displays emotions, despite having no limbs or face.*
© Disney

9

During the Second World War, box office revenues shrank, and the studio had to put ideas for more ambitious storytelling on hold. Disney continued producing feature-length package films, which consisted of a number of shorts. Clark continued animating on film titles like *Make Mine Music* and *Song of the South*, but it wasn't until *Fun and Fancy Free* that he found a signature assignment. The *Mickey and the Beanstalk* segment featured an unusual character, the Singing Harp. This combination of fairy and musical instrument presented the animator with limitations as far as motion goes. Only her upper body could move, the rest was attached to the wooden harp. Clark used elegant arm movements, as she points out to Mickey where Willie the Giant hid the key that is needed to free Goofy and Donald. Subtle, beautiful drawing and graceful animation made this unique character memorable.

Another curious assignment came along with the film *Melody Time*. It featured a section called *Bumble Boogie*, a jazzed up version of Rimsky-Korsakov's composition "The Flight of The Bumble Bee." This bee character flies through a "musical nightmare," as the narrator explains at the short film's opening. In his animation, Les Clark needed to keep up with the score's high energy and rhythm.

The visuals are among the most surreal scenes ever animated at Disney. The bee is being pursued and attacked by unfriendly flowers, musical instruments, and abstract lines. At one point during the chase he decides to fight back and brings this horrid dream to an end. There isn't much character development involved, but Clark still makes us feel sympathetic toward the little bee.

Clark created a memorable character in the Singing Harp from Mickey and the Beanstalk.
© Disney

Appealing design and energetic timing helped to make this tiny character come alive.
© Disney

Almost being cast against type, Les Clark joined colleagues Eric Larson and Marc Davis in animating the very realistic and beautiful *Cinderella*. The live-action reference, featuring actress Helene Stanley, proved to be both helpful and a curse. The footage provided the animators with acting patterns, but how should these movements by a real woman be translated into successful graphic motion on paper? There is an essence, an emotional core that needs to be found and enhanced for an animated character. Among many scenes with the film's title character, Clark animated her delivering an invitation from the palace to her stepmother. When the letter is being read out loud, Cinderella finds out that every eligible maiden is to attend the royal ball. She states, "That means I can go, too." Her stepmother plays along and responds, "If you find something suitable to wear!" The following scene shows Cinderella with such relief and joy, she is alive in the most convincing way. Her emotional state could not have been drawn and animated any better, as she says, "Oh, thank you, stepmother," before exiting. There is a truth and honesty in the way Clark handled the scene, as if he felt the character's hope and joy.

Clark's animation of Cinderella proved that he was perfectly able to deal with difficult, realistic assignments.
© Disney

11

His strong animation of Cinderella led to Clark's involvement with Disney's next leading lady, Alice from the film *Alice in Wonderland*. The technique would be similar, making intelligent use of live-action reference footage in order to present a young girl dealing with adverse situations.

One of his sequences shows Alice growing dramatically in size inside the White Rabbit's house, to a point where her arms and legs are sticking out of doors and windows. This presented certain staging challenges. On the one hand, Alice needed to look uncomfortable and awkward under these circumstances and, on the other hand, she needed to fit into this small house in a believable way.

Dramatic perspectives on humans are not an easy thing to achieve, but Clark's talents as a draftsman helped to present unusual up and down shots very successfully.

Clark tackled the challenge of fitting an enormous Alice into the White Rabbit's house.
© *Disney*

Having worked well with Marc Davis before, Les Clark joined his colleague again to help animate scenes with Tinker Bell, the emotional fairy in the film *Peter Pan*. While Davis did her introductory scenes, Clark drew Tinker Bell after she accidentally ends up trapped in a drawer. When Wendy charms Peter Pan during conversation, Tink knows that she is not going to like this girl. In a close-up scene, we see her lifting up a thimble very slowly to reveal her face. She literally turns red, full of jealousy.

Even though Marc Davis supervised the animation of Tinker Bell, Les Clark did not mind being the second-in-command.
© Disney

After a string of animated female characters, Les Clark switched gears on his next assignment for the film *Lady and the Tramp*. We see his work very early on in the film when Lady as a puppy refuses to be separated from her new owners at night. During several attempts, Jim Dear tries to make Lady stay downstairs by locking her in a room, but she finds new ways to break free. A daunting staircase separates her from the humans' bedroom upstairs. Undeterred, she goes on the daunting uphill journey, one step at a time. Clark's charming animation contains all the clumsiness of a real puppy. Her feet can't quite keep up with her movements. Being so young she is still uncoordinated, and that is where the entertainment lies. With each jump up the stairs her feet slip once or twice, which shows great determination to get to where she wants to be.

Eventually she reaches the upstairs bedroom, and from then on sleeps on the bed next to the Dears.

Clark's final animation before moving into other areas of animated film production.
© *Disney*

Walt Disney chose three of his Nine Old Men to become sequence directors for his ambitious production of *Sleeping Beauty*. They were Eric Larson, Woolie Reitherman, and Les Clark.

As older directors were retiring, it was time to fill those top spots with artists who knew animation and Disney's philosophy about filmmaking. Among the sequences Clark directed was the very complex opening of the film. Big crowds make their move toward King Stefan's castle to take part in Princess Aurora's birthday celebration. According to scene planner Ruthie Thomson, those scenes were the most difficult to coordinate, partly because of so many different cel levels. Maleficent's powerful entrance is also a part of the sequence. After *Sleeping Beauty*, Eric Larson went back to animation, Woolie Reitherman stayed on as director and eventually producer of Disney feature films, and Les Clark was put in charge of directing special projects like the educational film *Donald in Mathmagic Land*. His last project was overseeing the 1974 production of *Man, Monsters and Mysteries*, an entertaining film about the Loch Ness Monster myth. Les Clark was the only artist from Walt's first generation of animators who kept up with the changes and demands at the studio throughout the decades. He knew early on that Disney wanted better-looking animation, often more realistic draftsmanship, and nuanced performances. Clark took advantage of all the in-house art classes on offer in order to better himself. Even in later years he would finish his work at the studio then drive to an evening school for courses in portrait and landscape painting. The level of artistry kept rising at Disney, and Les Clark made every effort to keep up and improve his skills. He is the least known of the Nine Old Men, but hopefully his body of work shown here will rectify this.

Flowers and Trees

1932
WOMAN TREE
CLEAN-UP ANIMATION
Sc. 48

What a challenge this assignment must have been; creating a female personality out of a tree wouldn't be an easy task. But Clark, who had earlier developed subtle feminine qualities for the character of Minnie Mouse, was perfectly cast. By bending the tree trunk according to human anatomy such as the hip, knees, and neck, he succeeds in achieving elegant poses that the audience identifies as a young woman.

© Disney

50

53

100

106

16

57

58

96

110

114

118

The Country Cousin

1936
ABNER MOUSE
CLEAN-UP ANIMATION
Sc. 14

After the mice cousins arrive in front of the oversized human buffet, city mouse Monty nibbles on a small piece of cheese in a fine dining manner. By contrast country mouse Abner grabs a piece of cheese bigger than his head, and shoves it into his mouth. As he chews, his full hamster-like cheeks squash and stretch severely in a demonstration of his enormous appetite. It is astounding to see how far Clark goes with expressions and volume shifts. By showing these bad, yet funny table manners a clear difference is established between these two characters.

18

*F*antasia

1940
THE SORCERER'S APPRENTICE
MICKEY MOUSE
CLEAN-UP ANIMATION
Seq. 7, Sc. 11

Scenes like this one prove that Les Clark was one of the best Mickey Mouse animators. Mickey's forceful actions show serious determination, yet there is still an element of humor present. He repeatedly rolls up his long sleeves because they get in the way of his gesturing. His oversized outfit is a metaphor for someone who is in over his head. Clark paid close attention to how Mickey's hands are drawn, since they are the primary force in the scene. They retain the expressiveness of human hands, even with one finger missing.

© *Disney*

33
PD

41
PD

45
PD

65
PD

71
PD

73
PD

91
PD

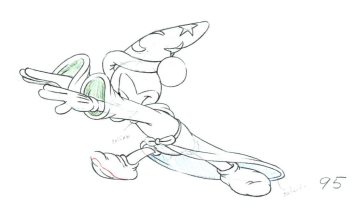

95

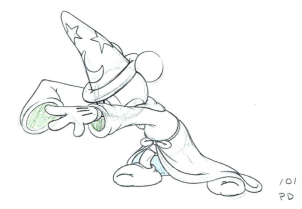

101
PD

54

57
PD

61
PD

75
PD

77
PD

85
PD

Symphony Hour

1942
MICKEY MOUSE
CLEAN-UP ANIMATION
Sc.6

Another beautiful piece of animation by Les Clark featuring Disney's most iconic character, as he conducts an orchestra. His extraverted gestures are perfectly timed to the music and are reminiscent of his performance in *Fantasia*.

At one point during the scene the music quiets down, and Mickey leans way forward in order to get closer to the orchestra. From a physical point of view he should actually fall down, because these poses are completely off-balance. Yet this exaggerated staging communicates that Mickey's movements are not limited by realism. As a cartoon character he can lower himself down toward his musicians as no live actor could. If the animation is entertaining the audience will believe it.

273 ©

283 ©

3/7 ©

325 ©

291©   301©   309©

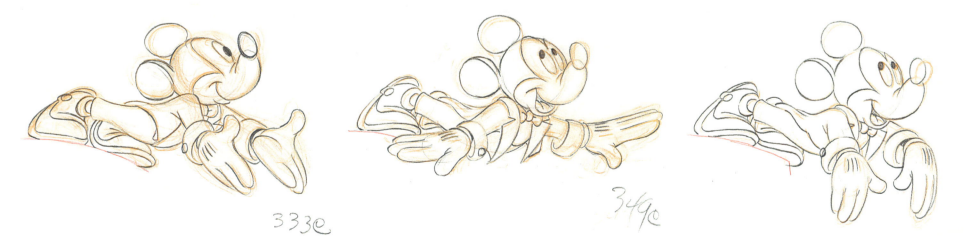

333©   349©   353©

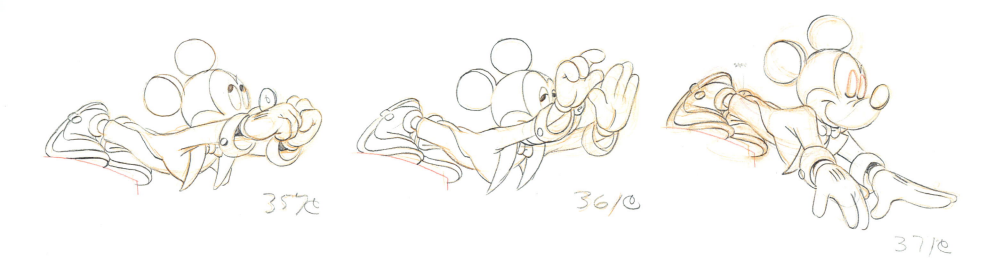

379©

387©

395©

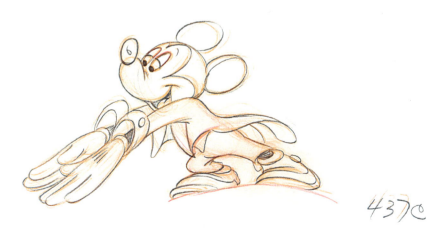

429

437©

Peter Pan

1953
WENDY
CLEAN-UP ANIMATION
Seq. 14, Sc. 102

Since all of Wendy's scenes were based on live-action reference, it was up to the animator to find the essence in the live performance and turn it into graphic motion.

Wendy along with her brothers and the Lost Boys celebrate the fact that Captain Hook admitted to being a codfish: "Hurray... Hook is a codfish, a codfish, a codfish..."

In this scene Clark is animating to the rhythm of the sung lines of dialogue. But there is something about Wendy's head tilts that show she is really enjoying Peter Pan's victory over Captain Hook in a kind of impish way.

© Disney

30

Wolfgang
Reitherman

When Walt Disney died in December of 1966, the world wondered what might happen to his animated film productions without Disney's leadership. The animators and other key personnel were concerned as well. Because of Walt's unexpected passing, the company was ill-prepared for a traumatic situation like this one. There were those in top management who thought the animation department should be shut down, after all the studio by then had amassed a large number of animated classics that could still generate income through rereleases. Animator/director Wolfgang Reitherman argued strongly for continuing animation, *The Jungle Book* was half-finished, and a new project called *The Aristocats* had been approved by Disney to move forward. Fortunately when *The Jungle Book* was released in October of 1967, it turned out to be a tremendous success and re-established Disney animation as a unique and valuable form of entertainment, loved the world over. Under Reitherman's leadership, the studio's group of master animators would produce a few more films until retirement age, but not before training a number of young artists that would help guarantee the future of the art form. Woolie Reitherman, as his colleagues called him, had made the switch from animator to co-director on the 1959 film *Sleeping Beauty*. At the time of Walt's death, he served as single director on the studio's animated features. Naturally his relationship with the other animators changed; formerly he had been a co-worker, now he was their boss. But this new arrangement worked (for the most part), because Woolie always insisted on teamwork, he had enormous respect for the talent in the department and key animators were included in important decisions regarding story and character development.

Throughout his life, Reitherman had been an enthusiastic pilot, he loved the feeling of freedom and independence in the cockpit. As a young man he was strong-willed with a zest for life and a sense of adventure. At the advice of an art teacher he applied to Disney and got hired in 1934.

The management at that time must have sensed Woolie's freewheeling spirit right away, because he was spared spending any time in the in-betweening department at all. Instead he jumped into animation right away and drew simple scenes on short films like *Funny Little Bunnies*, *Two-Gun Mickey*, and *The Band Concert*. Woolie stated later that he would not have survived the tedious assistant program for newcomers to the studio.

He was ready to take this new medium of animation straight on. Other short film assignments followed, and when Reitherman animated a few outstanding personality scenes with the character of Goofy for *Hawaiian Holiday*, his colleagues took notice. Just about every possible surfing mishap is shown here, with Goofy facing the additional challenge of trying to surf a wave that has a personality and doesn't like surfers. Timing is all-important in animated situations like these. Pauses within the action give the audience time to take in a gag and have a laugh.

Woolie's work on Hawaiian Holiday *made his colleagues take notice.*
© Disney

But Woolie's first assignment on an animated feature film would not get any laughs from the audience: the Magic Mirror in *Snow White and the Seven Dwarfs* served a purely dramatic purpose. When being asked a question by the evil Queen, he answers her truthfully. The Mirror is neither for nor against the Queen, his responses are delivered in a stern but neutral manner.

After animating a hilarious situation involving Goofy, this character's handling needed a completely different approach. The technical challenge Woolie faced was to draw the face in perfect symmetry. After several failed attempts, he came up with the idea to draw one half of the Mirror's face, then fold the paper and trace the other half. It took a lot of precision to give the right amount of life to this art deco face. Too much squash and stretch would have given a humorous, cartoony appearance, but not enough shape-change in the eyes and mouth, and the scenes would have turned out lifeless. After all that careful work, Reitherman was disappointed to see that the final film footage showed his character mostly covered up by fire and smoke effects.

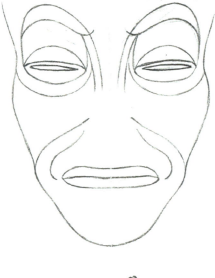

320

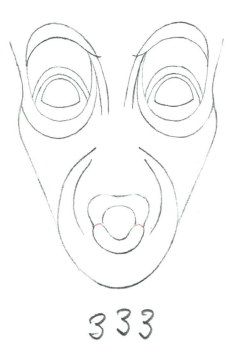

333

To make the Magic Mirror's face perfectly symmetrical, Woolie drew one half and then traced the other.
© Disney

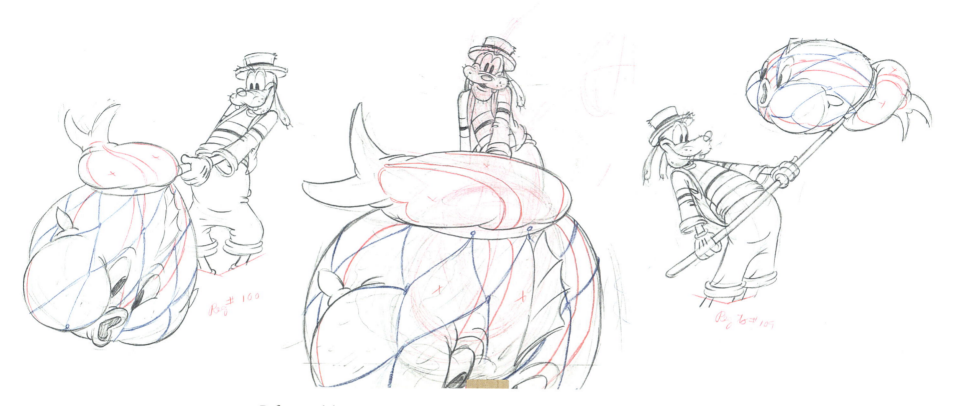

Before work began on Disney's second animated feature, Woolie had again the opportunity to hone his skills as an animator of comedy. In the 1939 short *Goofy and Wilbur* his animation is so gutsy and loose, it looks like Reitherman is shaking off any restrictions he had to deal with when animating the Magic Mirror. Goofy goes on a fishing expedition, and uses his grasshopper friend Wilbur as bait. At one point he finds himself in a state of panic when his friend gets swallowed by a fish. The amazing looseness in Goofy's movements is partly the result of the animator's use of baggy clothing in secondary action. Sleeves, vest, and pants all hang limp on the character's body. When he moves, these materials drag and help the overall flow of the animation.

Woolie applied a real sense of perspective to Goofy's animation. An arm motion gets close to camera and is drawn considerably larger to achieve a feeling of dimension and depth.
© Disney

37

The same year saw the release of the short *Donald's Cousin Gus*. Woolie animated the character Gus Goose, who visits Donald and brings along a colossal appetite. The film opens with the arrival of Gus at Donald's home, and right away his screen presence is utterly captivating. From his unconventional, bouncy walk to the way he comes to a stop in an off-balanced pose, this character's pantomime performance is inventive and entertaining. Woolie again drew certain moves using exaggerated perspective, as Gus makes a sweeping turn to face the entrance of Donald's home. First one of his feet gets close to camera, followed by his arm holding a travel bag. This whole rotation adds believability as well as comedy to the performance.

Cousin Gus comes to life through Reitherman's unique ideas for comical acting.
© *Disney*

Woolie proved that he had become an animator with great versatility, when he began work on Monstro, the whale for the feature *Pinocchio*. His talent for funny personality animation needed to be put aside, this character was a true monster who would not only terrify Pinocchio and Geppetto but audiences as well. He was also the climax of the film, and much excitement and fear needed to be developed in order to contrast the emotions of the happy ending that followed.

Monstro presented many drawing and animation challenges. How can this creature that has the square shape of an oversized school bus be brought to life? What kind of a motion range should he have? Woolie broke up the whale's body into three main volumes: head, body, and tail. During dramatic moves—particularly turns—those body parts could be twisted and offset, resulting in dynamic poses and motion. When drawn from low camera angles, Monstro did indeed come across as monstrous. The choice of perspective makes all the difference in such a situation. When looking up at a creature, it becomes instantly imposing and massive looking. Instead, when looking down on to it, the creature seems less frightening, because the viewer is placed at a higher, safer level. While Monstro's overall body shape looks fairly simple, Reitherman added detail wherever possible. The whale's fleshy mouth with its countless teeth as well as the definition of his whole underside helped to give the illusion of scale. Staging became critically important.

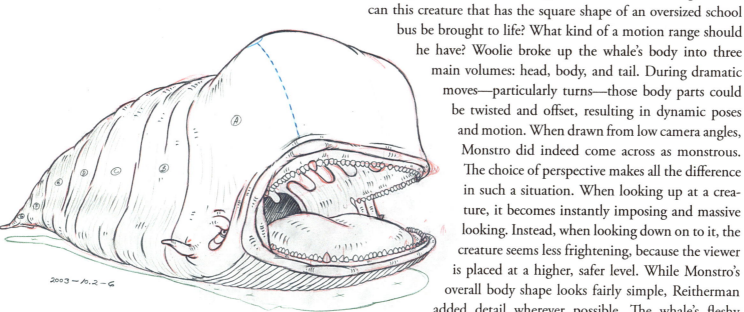

Reitherman captures the enormous scale of Monstro.
© Disney

Certain scenes showed the entire body, while others were framed closer, so that other characters could fit into the frame. The pacing of the sequence's editing had to keep building up to the final two scenes in which Monstro leaps right into camera before crashing into rocks on the shoreline. No other action/chase sequence in Disney animation compares to the high drama of this spectacle at sea.

39

Scale and size were most definitely a major consideration in Woolie's next assignment for animating the epic battle of a Tyrannosaurus Rex and a Stegosaur in *Fantasia*'s "Rite of Spring" sequence. Stravinsky's music set the tone for this ferocious fight to the death. The problem was, how do you bring to life creatures that are extinct? What kind of research would tell you how they might have moved? The place to study prehistoric creatures like these was the Los Angeles National History Museum. Skeletons of dinosaurs gave Reitherman useful information about how the ancient animals were built on the inside. How this knowledge would translate into graphic motion became the animator's judgment call. Woolie realized that a T-Rex could not possibly have fought using his small arms, instead his enormous teeth were his main weapon. During a walk, the gigantic legs—carrying all that weight—would make the ground shudder on contact. The Stegosaur by contrast had short legs and could only take small steps, as he tried to back away from the aggressor. It took tremendous analysis to achieve natural-looking movements for this monumental fight. On top of that, the animation needed to be in sync with the intense music. On scenes like these, Woolie usually started by putting intuitive scribbles on paper that showed initial compositions and forces. He would then rework and refine those sketches several times over, until he saw believable action that represented what he was aiming for. Fellow animator Ollie Johnston once stated that Woolie sent out more tests to be photographed for a given scene than anybody else. Just like a sculptor, he felt the character's raw forms first, before any details were added.

FACING PAGE
By blocking in the dinosaurs' anatomy, Woolie gained control over their colossal body masses and perspective.
© Disney

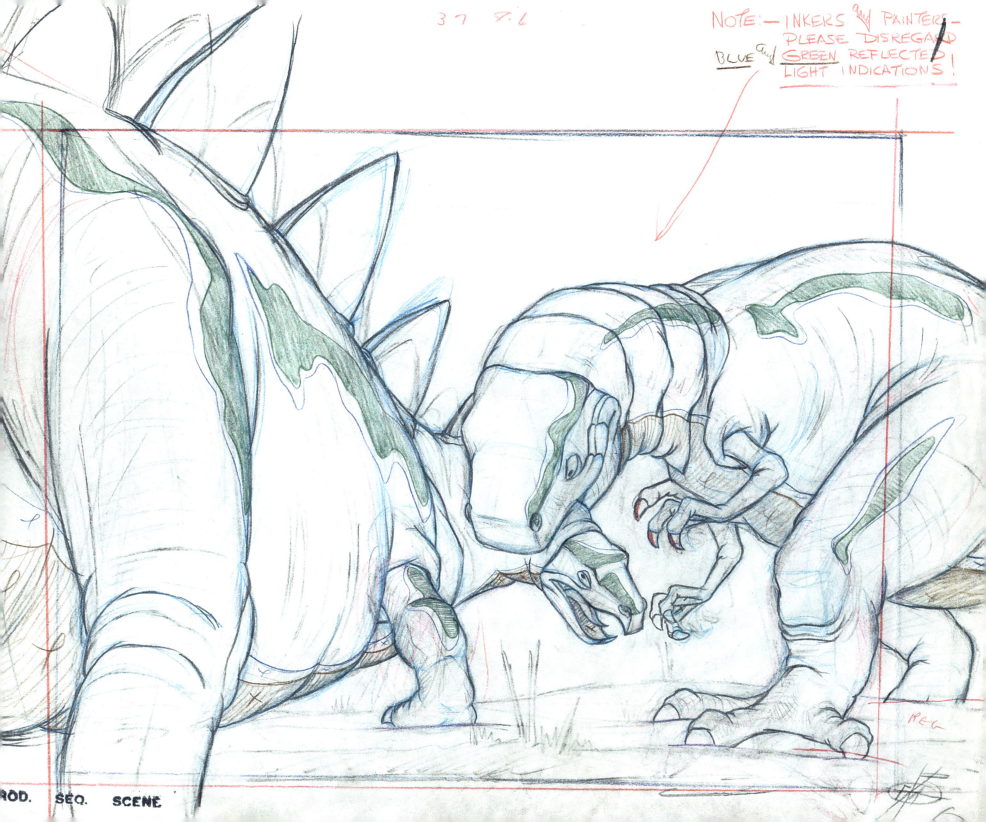

It is astonishing to witness Reitherman's ability to switch from very dramatic animation like the "Rite of Spring" to hilarious character acting like *The Reluctant Dragon*. He animated the dragon's opening scenes as he meets the boy from the village. His performance is over-the-top, flamboyant, and very entertaining. We know right away that this dragon is not the fighting type, he prefers writing poetry. What is so surprising is that Woolie's superb animation fits in seamlessly with Ward Kimball's wacky concept for the character. Two animators with different backgrounds and sensibilities come together and create one of the funniest Disney characters. Reitherman also animated on another section of the film, featuring Goofy in *How to Ride a Horse*. This was natural casting because of his earlier experiences with the character.

Woolie's talents range from realistic drama to outrageous comedy.
© Disney

There was one type of personality Woolie had not tried to animate yet. Sweet sympathetic characters were usually handed to animators like Ollie Johnston, Frank Thomas, or Fred Moore.

But for some reason, important introductory scenes of Timothy Mouse in the film *Dumbo* were assigned to Woolie. After watching the little pachyderm being rejected by other circus elephants, the mouse decides to investigate the situation and tries to befriend Dumbo, who is hiding in a haystack. We find out that Timothy is quite the psychiatrist, because after a short talk, during which he introduces himself as a friend, the elephant comes out of hiding to meet the friendly rodent. Timothy is an anthropomorphic mouse, he wears clothes, walks on two legs, and gestures like a human. What is interesting to see is that he maintains mouse-like qualities. Woolie's animation shows quick moves and appealing poses that communicate what sort of character he is: a buddy, who is there for you. His walk needed to be established in this early section of the film. At one point Timothy turns away from Dumbo in order to fake a momentary disinterest in the elephant's problem. The movement of his little legs have just the right amount of rotation so that an audience believes, if a mouse could walk on two legs, this is what it would look like.

A mouse that walks like a human looking like a mouse.
© *Disney*

43

*The chase sequence in
The Legend of Sleepy
Hollow had dramatic
action, interspersed with
pauses for the audience to
catch their breath.*
© Disney

After *Dumbo* was finished, Disney was no longer able to continue feature-length productions. *Pinocchio* and *Fantasia* had not generated profits during their original releases, while overseas markets were cut off because of the war. The studio managed to stay afloat by turning out propaganda and other short films. Woolie contributed beautiful animation to films like *El Gaucho Goofy, How to Swim* and *How to Fish*. But for the next few years he left the studio to fly for the United States Air Force. Woolie would not return to Disney until April 1947. The studio had begun work on two featurette films *The Wind in the Willows* and *The Legend of Sleepy Hollow*.

The latter included a dramatic chase sequence that involved the frightening Headless Horseman in pursuit of the main character Ichabod Crane. Woolie was back in his element as an animator of exciting action scenes. On Halloween night, Ichabod rides home after attending a party. The sounds of the forest become more and more daunting when, out of nowhere, the Headless Horseman appears with only one thing in mind, to cut off Ichabod's head with his sword. There are occasional comedic moments during the sequence (Ichabod's horse is clumsy and as frightened as his rider), but for the most part this chase is exhilarating and relentless. Woolie strongly believed in pacing an action sequence a certain way. He stated that during fast-paced action scenes there needs to be pauses where things slow down. This would give viewers the chance to catch their breath before tension rises again and speed is accelerated again. The Headless Horseman's steed takes a big leap into the air, which slows down the running pattern. Horse and rider then land downhill and pick up the pursuit. Another pause in the action occurs when Ichabod hangs on to the neck of his galloping horse. He is smiling and petting the horse's head, because he believes the danger has passed. Moments like these help to give texture to a volatile sequence.

Exciting material kept coming Woolie's way. For the film *Cinderella* he animated the climactic scenes with the mice Gus and Jaq, as they try to deliver a key to Cinderella, who has been locked up in her room. The task seems overwhelming because they need to pull the key up an extremely high staircase. Tension is increased by the cat, Lucifer, who interferes with the mission of the brave mice. At any given moment during the sequence the chance of making it all the way to the top of the tower seems impossible. The filmmakers cut back and forth to a different situation downstairs, where the Grand Duke is visiting with the stepsisters and Lady Tremaine, who is unaware of the missing key. Editing, pacing, and a feeling of anxiety make this one of the most suspenseful sequences ever put on film.

Less dramatic but more surreal was Reitherman's assignment for *Alice in Wonderland*. He animated the sequence where the White Rabbit unsuccessfully tries to prevent his house from being destroyed by Alice. The girl has magically grown to the size of a giant after entering the cottage. Now her huge arms and legs squeeze through doors and windows, threatening the structure's foundation. The bizarre storytelling doesn't prove very captivating, so Woolie focused on establishing contrasts between the involved characters. Alice only wants to regain her actual size, while the nervous lizard tries to follow orders from the bossy dodo, who tells him to go

Woolie emphasizes the weight of the large key, an almost unmanageable obstacle.
© Disney

45

down the chimney to get rid of the human monster. It is hard to get to know those two characters since their appearance in the film is very brief. But the White Rabbit is entertaining and shows consistency in his personality. During all the commotion around his house, he keeps pointing at his watch, afraid of being too late. We never find out what for.

The White Rabbit is in constant fear of being late.
© Disney

Woolie found much more satisfaction animating scenes with Captain Hook for the next film, *Peter Pan*. His colleague Frank Thomas supervised the animation of the character, but was unable to draw every single scene with him. It was decided that Reitherman had the perfect experience to handle an action sequence that included the encounter between Captain Hook and the Crocodile. Applying broad action combined with brilliant comedy, Woolie turned this sequence into the most thrilling section of the film. Nothing seemed to be off limits. The Crocodile swallows the Captain whole, before he re-emerges intact. During a tense moment, Hook tries to prevent being eaten by standing at the edge

of the creature's mouth, holding it open with all his might. Those scenes raised a few eyebrows at the studio; after all, such cartoony situations had previously been reserved for a character like Goofy. Woolie did not care; he had too much fun making the impossible come off as believable. Audiences turned out to be on his side; they bought the bizarre animation, because it was entertaining. And what kept it from looking like a Goofy short was the fact that Woolie always drew Hook with accurate human anatomy. This broad sequence actually added to the range of Hook's personality. He is definitely a menace to Peter Pan, but in this instance he almost gets consumed by an oversized crocodile. Even villains live in fear.

Reitherman said: *"Nobody is going to worry about a gag's logic, if it's funny."*
© Disney

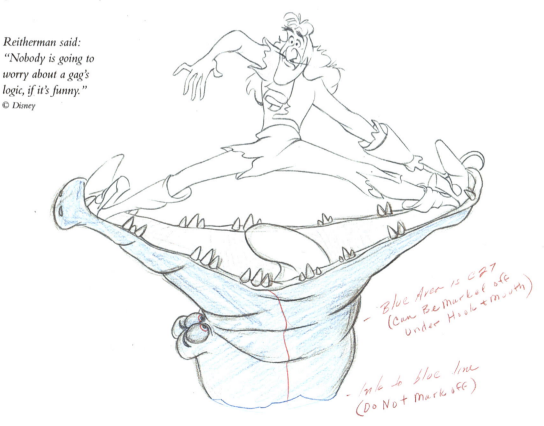

Broad action, but in a solely dramatic way was required for two major sequences in the movie *Lady and the Tramp*. Woolie's animation brought thrilling excitement to both sections of the film. After Lady runs away from Aunt Sarah, she is being chased by a pack of street dogs. When they corner her, Tramp comes to the rescue and fights them off. The fact that he is outnumbered makes for an intense situation. Before the fight begins, Tramp stares the dogs down, as he growls in a frozen position. The actual combat doesn't last very long and is partially staged as shadows. A few fierce close ups of dogs biting add to the feeling of heightened emotion. After the dogs flee, Tramp, out of breath, turns his attention to Lady who had been hiding behind a barrel.

During this fight sequence, realistic drawing was required to make the action believable.
© *Disney*

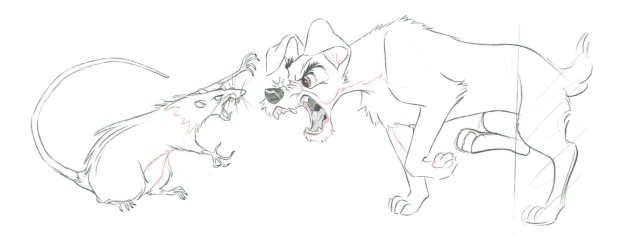

Woolie's other action sequence takes place at the end of the film, when Tramp enters the house to confront a rat that has approached the baby's cradle. Woolie timed this fight as dramatically as he could. Rat and dog face each other, moving ever so slightly, then in a flash their movements become fast and jerky… and suddenly they freeze again. Tramp ends the confrontation with one quick bite. By now Woolie had become a true master at dramatic action, a role that would continue into the next film.

Real drama as Tramp fights the rat.
© *Disney*

As mentioned, Reitherman became a sequence director on *Sleeping Beauty*. His days as an animator were over. Now Woolie would have greater control over certain sections of the film by working closely with story people and layout artists to get the maximum out of a sequence. One of them dealt with the epic confrontation between Prince Phillip and the Dragon. He supervised all of the animation that was done for this dramatic encounter.

"Now shall you deal with me, my prince, and all the powers of hell" are Maleficent's final words as she transforms herself into a terrifying dragon. It was important for Woolie that the audience believed the beast is going to kill the prince. After a few fire-breathing threats, the pursuit begins and steadily intensifies. Phillip is fighting as he backs away through thorns, up a hill, until there is nowhere to go. Just when it looks like the end for the prince, he throws his sword into the dragon's heart. Fire effects animation and the intense musical score based on Tchaikovsky help to keep the audience on the edge of their seats throughout the sequence. Unfortunately the film lost money in its initial release, it seems audiences could not warm up to a film this stylized.

The following film, *One Hundred and One Dalmatians* (1961) represented a significant change in Disney storytelling. After the monumental production of the fairy tale *Sleeping Beauty*, *Dalmatians* was set in contemporary London. No pixie dust or magic anywhere in sight, this story was about the kidnapping of puppies. Reitherman was one of three co directors, who translated Bill Peet's storyboard into the first Disney film of the modern era. Gone were the lush, realistically painted backgrounds, making room for a fresh, cutting-edge visual style. One of the sequences Woolie directed was the utterly charming twilight bark. Desperate to let the word out about their puppies'

Eric Cleworth animated many scenes for the fight under Woolie's direction.
© Disney

50

disappearance, Pongo and Perdita use this canine gossip line to reach other dogs in a call for help. *One Hundred and One Dalmatians* was made for a fraction of *Sleeping Beauty*'s cost, the film was enormously successful worldwide, and proved that Disney animated films could be profitable again.

Starting with *The Sword in the Stone*, Woolie served as solo director. Walt Disney had gotten to a point where he trusted Woolie's judgment and experience. Since Walt had gotten involved with many other types of entertainment (theme parks, TV) that took much of his time, it was important to him that an artist with natural leadership skills took on his animated productions.

The Sword in the Stone proved fairly unsuccessful with critics as well as audiences, but *The Jungle Book* broke studio box office records. The tone of the stories being told in Disney films by then was much milder than in Walt's earlier achievements. Woolie wanted to make films for families, and he became increasingly concerned about scaring children with terrifying villains.

He stated around that time: "If we lose the kids, we've lost everything." Perhaps raising his own children made him change his philosophy for storytelling. What kind of animated films would he want his three sons to see? Films that followed like *The Aristocats*, *Robin Hood*, and *The Rescuers* all had comedic villains and rich character relationships. All of them were successful and laid the foundation for a new generation of animation artists to put their mark on the art form. Woolie Reitherman was not only one of the world's top animators, he also made sure that Disney animation would continue on into the new century.

Donald's Cousin Gus

1939
GUS
CLEAN-UP ANIMATION OVER ROUGH
ANIMATION
Sc. 4

One of Disney's greatest characters in short films is Gus, a cousin of Donald, who shows up out of the blue with a huge appetite. Woolie sets up this odd, but fun-loving character right from the start as he arrives in front of Donald's house. The mailbox confirms that he is in the right place, and it's time to approach the front door behind him. Gus anticipates his little stroll by lifting one foot way up high before swinging it toward the camera, then away from it. As his upper body turns around, the hand holding his travel bag does the same foreshortening motion. Woolie's animation drawings move within real space. The strong use of squash and stretch during his walk away from the viewer turns this scene into a comical masterpiece.

52

57

57A

69

71

53

77

81

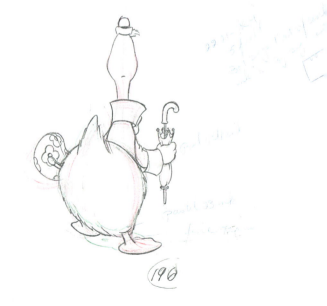

189B

193

196

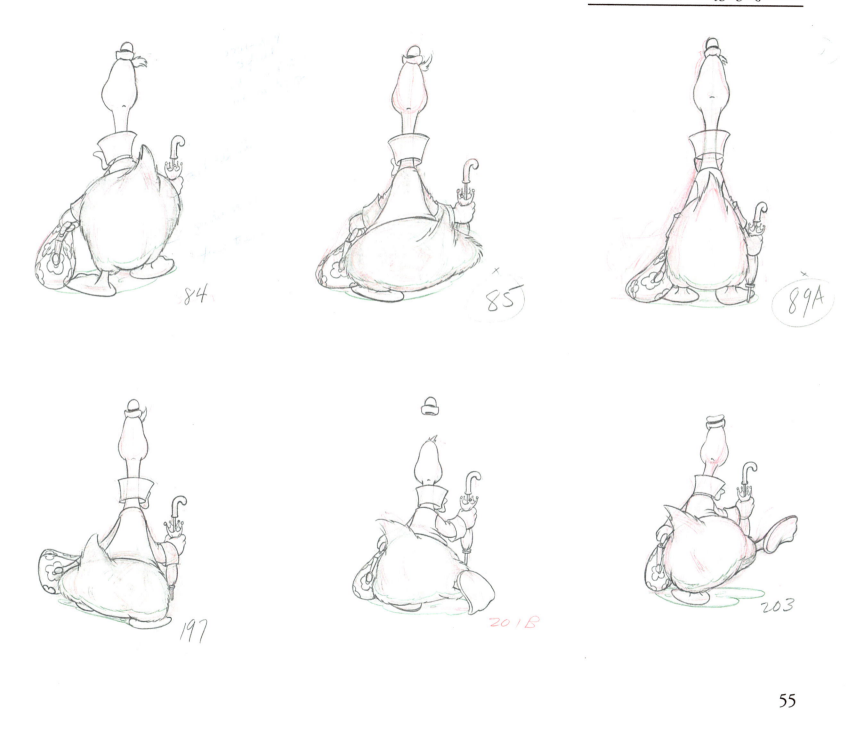

84

85

89A

197

201B

203

Pinocchio

1940
MONSTRO
CLEAN-UP OVER ROUGH ANIMATION
Seq. 10.9, Sc. 8

Monstro is accelerating his pursuit of the little raft holding Pinocchio, Geppetto, Figaro, and Cleo. He makes a huge turn upward toward the surface by almost brushing the camera. One after the other, each main body part approaches the viewer, first the head with its open mouth, followed by the middle frame and the tail. Woolie effectively animated this move from a low eye-level, which increases the drama and emotion of the scene.

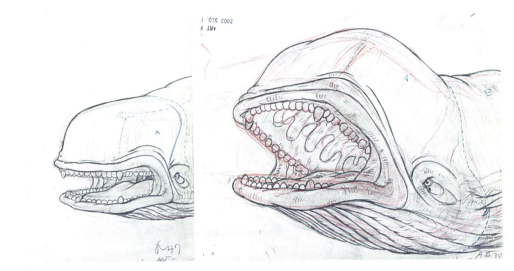

© Disney

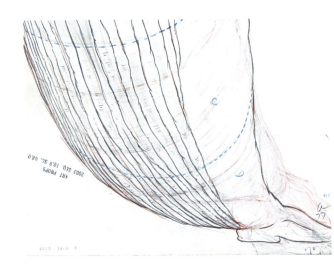
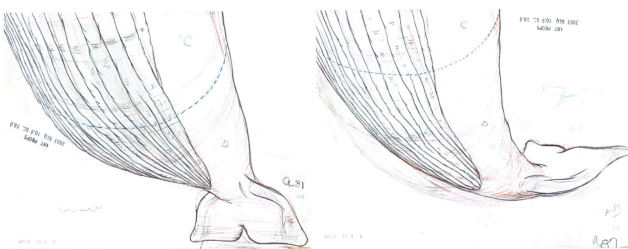

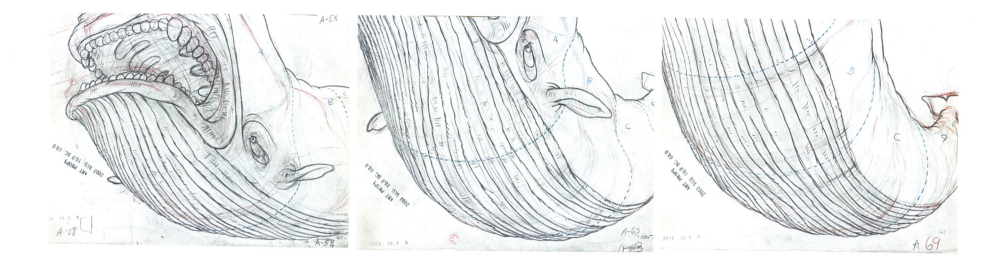

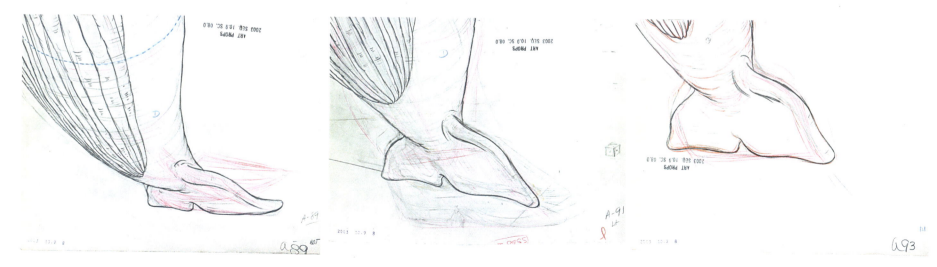

*F*antasia

1940
"RITE OF SPRING"
TYRANNOSAURUS REX
CLEAN-UP OVER ROUGH ANIMATION
Seq. 8.6, Sc. 43

During the "Rite of Spring" section, a horrific Tyrannosaurus Rex is about to lurch toward a Stegosaur. Woolie has the prehistoric monster lean back in anticipation of his leap into the camera. It is important to give a heavy creature like this one plenty of time to change directions, otherwise the animation would lack weight. In this case the T-Rex hovers about ten frames at his high point, before rapidly approaching the camera. There is no better way to frighten an audience than to make it feel that a giant beast is coming down on them.

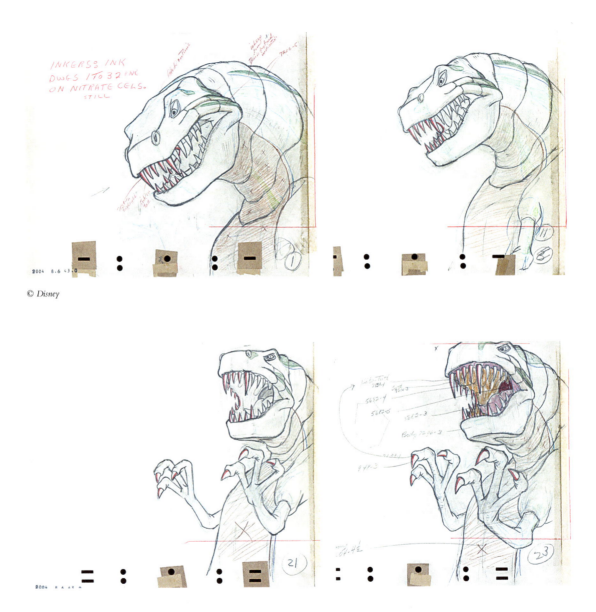

58

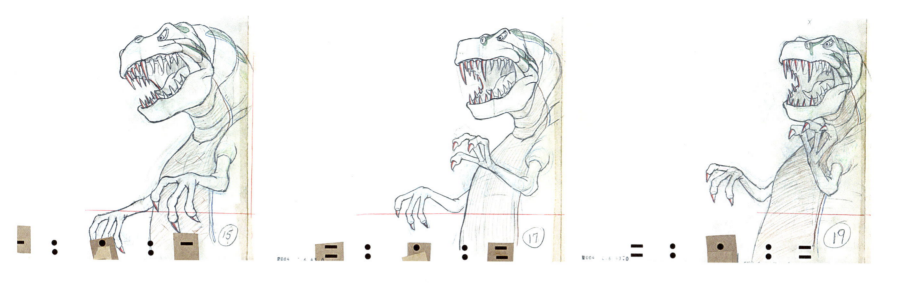

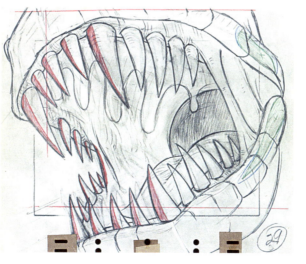

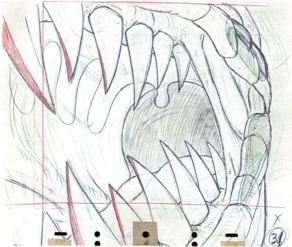

Saludos Amigos

1943
EL GAUCHO GOOFY
GOOFY AND HORSE
CLEAN-UP OVER ROUGH ANIMATION
Sc. 37

In full gaucho outfit, Goofy is riding his horse in pursuit of an ostrich. He seems to be an expert hunter; within seconds he catches the bird. When the film rewinds to the start of the hunt, the scene is shown again, but in extreme slow motion. At this slow speed the audience is supposed to become aware of Goofy's professional and impressive technique. What we watch instead is a series of hilarious mishaps as Goofy bounces up and down the horse in cartoony fashion before making a painful landing on his own spurs. Woolie exaggerated every piece of action as much as he could, and applied squash and stretch more severely than he normally would, because he knew that it would look funny. These highly detailed key drawings required a humongous amount of in-betweens in order to present the action this slowly. Woolie must have worked with the studio's most patient assistant.

© Disney

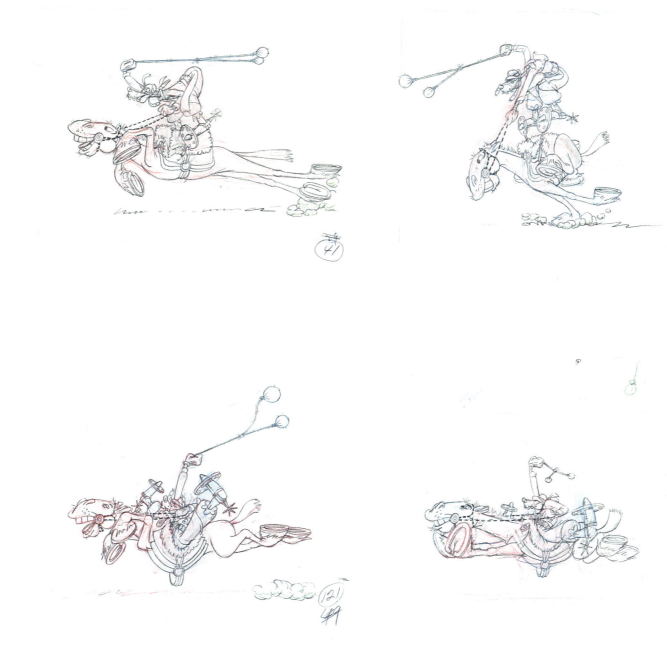

185

209

241

305

313

321

The Adventures of Ichabod and Mr. Toad

1949
ICHABOD AND KATRINA
CLEAN-UP ANIMATION
Seq. 7, Sc. 21

Ichabod is doing his best to impress Katrina Van Tassel at the party. Woolie's funny animation of the couple shows them holding relatively still, while Ichabod's gangly legs keep kicking up out of nowhere. His crazy footwork becomes the center of comedy for the scene. It isn't until moments later that the characters change into a more conventional dancing pattern. As good as Woolie was handling dramatic material, his comedy scenes rank among the best ever done at the studio.

© Disney

29

31

32

41

Eric Larson

"***W**alt Disney* never talked down to an audience, instead he always tried to bring you up to his level." Those words by animator Eric Larson were directed at young newcomers to the studio during the early 1980s, people like Mark Henn and Ruben Aquino, as well as this author. Eric tried to make it clear to us that top quality work was key to any Disney animated production. He talked about having high standards in your work as a good rule to live by and a good way to express yourself as an animator. In so many ways Eric was much more than an animation teacher; he represented the Disney philosophy of bringing things to life in a believable, genuine way. There were certainly useful tools of the trade that were a big part of his curriculum, but no matter how frustrated we occasionally became with our early attempts to animate—poor timing and the lack of weight showed our inexperience—a talk with Eric always left us with a feeling that this is the greatest art form in the world. We all knew what a privilege it was to be a part of a group of artists that was encouraged to continue the traditions of Disney animation under the guidance of one of the medium's masters.

This quote from one of Eric's lectures exemplifies his affection for animated filmmaking:

> Animation is a form of communication, and therefore when you're animating you are making a statement: a statement about the character, the story, the feelings and emotions, actions, personalities, archetypes, etc. If you want the audience to get involved in the story, connect with the character, and feel the emotions needed to sympathize and relate to that character you must make a positive statement. To make a positive statement you have to know your characters and their personality, have a devotion to your craft, know how to use your art to express the statement you want to make, apply feelings and emotions that are strong and real to a fantasy story, and most of all have sincerity. If you don't have feelings and emotions for your character, how can it even be possible for the audience to?

Young Eric Larson originally pursued writing with the hopes of becoming a journalist. But he also enjoyed drawing, and when in the early 1930s word got around that Walt Disney was hiring artists Eric applied and was hired as an in-betweener. He did assistant work on short films like *Two-Gun Mickey*, *Mickey's Service Station*, and the groundbreaking *The Tortoise and the Hare*, which featured innovative action scenes by animator Ham Luske. At one point the Hare plays tennis with himself, speeding back and forth on the tennis court.

Luske had to work hard to make his drawings look good, and to make them perform in a way that felt believable and genuine to him. Eric was not a natural draughtsman either and often struggled to catch up with animators like Milt Kahl or Marc Davis, whose work was always beautifully drawn and showed a flair for strong design. But to Eric the struggle was worth the effort to get a performance on the screen. And it was certainly not beneath him to ask superior draftsmen at the studio for help in order to make his scenes look better. This kind of teamwork was very much encouraged by Walt Disney himself, who knew that his artists could learn from each other, particularly when the studio started work on their first feature-length production *Snow White and the Seven Dwarfs*. It was at that time that Eric got his big break. At the suggestion of Ham Luske, Eric was promoted to full-fledged animator. He joined Milt Kahl in animating large groups of forest animals who interacted with Snow White in many scenes. This was a hugely labor-intensive assignment. To synchronize the movements of several deer, chipmunks, and bunnies has more to do with choreographing a ballet than animating your

Eric Larson was very much impressed by the way Ham Luske timed his actions. For very fast motions speed lines were drawn to simulate a motion blur. It might have been slightly overdone, but this experiment succeeded in creating fast but smooth-looking animation.
© Disney

71

average scene. Real animal motion needed to be studied so that the animation would look natural enough next to the realistic character of Snow White. Eric was happy with most of the results; however, he felt that the deer—with their flour-sack bodies—could have benefitted from a dose of strong anatomy.

Synchronizing so many woodland creatures was more like choreographing a ballet than animating a scene.
© Disney

72

*Rooster and hen in the
middle of a romantic duet.*
© Disney

Before getting involved in Disney's second animated
feature, Eric continued working on charming, cartoony
animal characters for short films like *Farmyard Symphony*
and *The Ugly Duckling*. The Disney style of the late 1930s
and 1940s had a soft, cuddly quality, and Eric felt very
comfortable with this relatively simple approach to drawing and constructing animated characters.

The Ugly Duckling is born.
© Disney

73

While these farm animals were designed in a simple way to tell a short story, Eric's next character needed to have a much more developed personality, after all he became one of the main characters in the film *Pinocchio*. Figaro's early designs were a caricature of an adult cat, but Eric much preferred to portray this mischievous, but lovable character as a kitten. His feline moves feel so believable because they are based on real cat motion and then caricatured in the most loving way. Figaro's human attributes and expressions have roots in a former Larson family member, Eric's four-year-old nephew. Kids that age show typical characteristics of misbehavior and mood swings but also affection for their parents, and Figaro's personality fits all of these attributes. Then there is a classic brother–sister relationship between him and the goldfish, Cleo. That kind of character pairing offers rich and contrasting situations that help to bring these youngsters to life. Eric produced some beautiful pantomime animation in an early section of the film. Geppetto and Figaro have just settled for the night into their respective beds, when the old woodcarver decides to make a wish. Geppetto asks Figaro to open the window so he can ask the wishing star for Pinocchio to become a real boy. Eric saw great potential in the way Figaro could react in this situation. He first looks up to Geppetto with an upset "Now what?" expression, then tosses his blanket with each foot at a time before tumbling out of bed in the direction of the window. He hops on to Geppetto's bed and crosses over a soft bedcover. Figaro's body reacts beautifully to each surface he comes in contact with. Strong squash drawing is used when he first tumbles out of his bed and hits the hard wooden floor. By contrast his legs sink deeply into Geppetto's bedcover, which communicates the weight of the cat as well as how cushy the blanket is. All this adds a ton of charm to this little character, who Eric obviously adored animating.

Figaro crossing a soft bedcover in the film Pinocchio.
© Disney

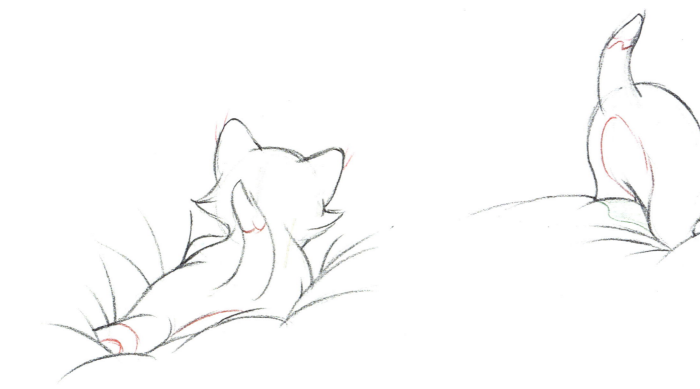

REG B G

A very different type of animation was required for Eric's other assignment on *Pinocchio*. Walt asked him to take over the marionettes that danced on Stromboli's stage and interacted with Pinocchio. These characters were not supposed to look alive, since their actions were manipulated by offstage humans. Eric knew that in order to make the audience believe that these puppets were made out of wood, a different approach to their animation was needed. Absolutely no squash and stretch was applied when their bodies hit the floor or made contact with each other. Wood is a very hard material, and distorting their volumes would have made them look like living characters. Eric synchronized the animation perfectly to the musical beats of the song "I've Got No Strings," and the result is an utterly convincing performance with marionettes.

A unique approach was required to make audiences believe the marionettes were made out of wood.
© Disney

Figaro's actions showed real feline motion while the stage puppets acted with no inner lives at all. Eric Larson's next assignment for Disney's *Fantasia* called for a fantastical and imagined type of movement, since the characters were centaurs. They appeared in the Beethoven/"Pastoral" sequence. This classic combination of horse and man presented a challenge in terms of body rhythm. How would the human upper body react to the motions of the lower horse anatomy and vice versa? Animator Fred Moore had designed these fantasy creatures in a simple, roundish, and cartoony way. So drawing them didn't present major difficulties, but making them move turned out to be the real challenge. That important unified body rhythm was never established in motion, and the end results look stiff.

Years later Eric talked to us students about the fact that he still felt embarrassed by his animation of those centaurs. "The girls look OK for the most part," he said, "but the men never come to life properly."

Eric Larson questioned the quality of the centaurs' design as well as his animation.
© Disney

77

Eric had more success with the flying horses in the "Pastoral" section of Fantasia.
© *Disney*

Eric redeemed himself, however, when he also animated several scenes with members of the Pegasus family in the same *Pastoral* section of *Fantasia*. The graceful movements of a flying horse needed to be invented as well, but Eric found this combination of bird and horse a much more pleasant assignment than the centaurs. There is great elegance in the way these huge creatures land softly in the water before their wings are turned backward to simulate floating swans.

After animating mythological flying animals, Eric turned to a "real" bird for the film *Bambi*. He developed and drew Friend Owl, a character he much identified with. Intentional or not, Eric's own gentle personality greatly influenced this owl's character, who

often shows fatherly affection towards the other forest animals. That is, until spring season arrives and the calm of the forest is interrupted by noisy birds and other "twitterpated" animals. His attempt to quiet everybody down with a loud warning is unsuccessful, and he flies off in search of a more peaceful part of the woods. What follows is an unexpected, but very entertaining performance that mocks the birds' courtship behavior: "Tweet, tweet! Pain in the pinfeathers I call it."

We find out that Friend Owl has a somewhat zany sense of humor.

Larson's own gentle character and sense of humor are reflected in the personality of Friend Owl.
© Disney

79

The character was voiced by actor Bill Wright who sounds like everybody's favorite grandfather. And that is exactly who Eric Larson became in his later years, a kind and patient mentor with an edgy sense of humor.

After *Bambi* and for the rest of the 1940s The Walt Disney Studios focused on the production of short films. Eric animated on several films with Goofy such as *Tiger Trouble* and *African Diary*.

The star of the short *The Flying Gauchito* was Burrito, a donkey with wings, and Eric again ended up drawing a Pegasus-like creature. Frank Thomas supervised the character's animation, and Eric was a natural choice to help out because of his experience with flying horses for *Fantasia*.

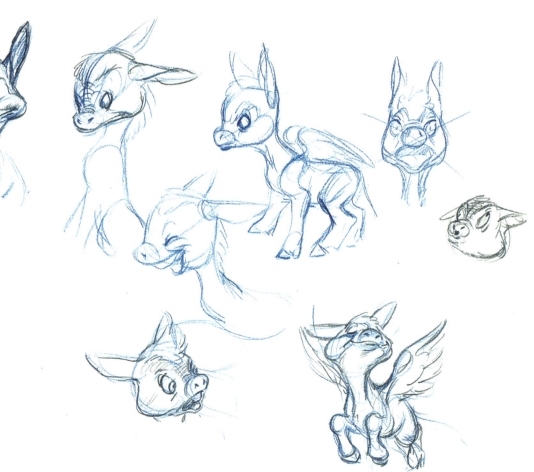

Eric researched a range of facial expressions as well as simplified horse and partial bird anatomy.
© Disney

80

By now Eric had become somewhat of an expert in animating birds. When work began on the short film *Peter and the Wolf*, he was cast on Peter's eccentric little bird friend Sasha. This character's emotions were always strong and extreme. When he first sees Peter, Sasha is very happy, and when he encounters the Wolf, he is very frightened. His movements are extremely fast and snappy. Eric would hold a pose for about ten frames, just enough to register, before quickly moving on to another pose. This kind of timing gave Sasha a nervous, energetic quality. He also comes across as enthusiastic and adventure-loving. After all, his friend Peter surely won't be able to track down the Wolf by himself.

Eric told his students later that at least eight frames of film are needed for any pose to read on the screen. Anything less than that would make the pose disappear in action.

Snappy timing was again needed for the main characters in the film *Song of the South*. Eric saw a lot of potential in developing rich personalities based on the voice recordings, which suggested a strong contrast between the slow bear, the fast fox, and the smart rabbit. Eric animated a scene in which Brer Rabbit is caught in the fox's trap. This is a very awkward position, and any acting is restricted to head turns and small hand gestures. But Eric still managed to portray the rabbit with the confidence that he could talk Brer Bear into freeing him.

A small character with big emotions.
© *Disney*

Brer Rabbit displaying unlimited confidence despite limited movement.
© *Disney*

81

Clips from this film were often shown during Eric's classes on action analysis. The animation is often at a very fast pace, but all poses and expressions read clearly. It taught us students just how far you can take personality animation in terms of speed and energy.

Just like on *Song of the South*, Eric Larson was one of a few supervising animators on the 1948 film *Melody Time*, which included several short films for a feature-length presentation. Eric did significant animation work on a couple of titles. One of them, *Once Upon a Wintertime*, is a simple love story, featuring Joe and Jenny, as they skate on the ice within a Mary Blair-inspired environment.

Stylized designs allowed for smooth, fluid animation.
© Disney

The two lovers get into an argument and almost separate before encountering the danger of breaking ice. But all ends well. Their character design is simple and graphically reminiscent of the fluid, rhythmic lines of caricaturist Al Hirschfeld. The animation reflects those design choices. Joe and Jenny move elegantly on the ice like professional skaters. Eric relished working on them, he found that their simple lines and shapes were easy to draw, which freed him up to focus on the animation. Animators who have difficulties drawing their characters will often produce stiff animation, because of the struggle they go through in putting a good pose or expression on paper.

Melody Time included another short film featuring beautiful Eric Larson animation. *Little Toot* is the name of a little tugboat with a mischievous, childlike personality. Eric said that when animating he thinks about those human qualities first, the fact that this character is an inanimate object is of a secondary nature. The story is again very simple: Because of his "show off" behavior Little Toot gets into trouble and is eventually banished out to the open sea. A storm rolls in, causing trouble for a vast liner nearby. After Little Toot pulls the huge ship to safety he is hailed a hero. Eric needed to bring the character's emotions across without the use of arms and legs. The main shape of the boat functions as a torso, and the cabin is drawn as a human head. Yet Eric was able to portray childlike attitudes by having the little boat hopping on the water, leaving splashes behind. Little Toot would wiggle his rear before moving forward at great speed. Moves like these are convincing because they are reminiscent of a happy kid or of a dog anticipating a jump. This was part of Eric's philosophy; personality animation needs to have roots in the artist's observation of real-life situations.

Little Toot manages to demonstrate childlike qualities, despite having no arms or legs.
© *Disney*

83

Eric Larson had to shift gears between a fantasy character like Little Toot and a realistic human like the title character in *Cinderella*. Studying live-action footage carefully was the basis for subtle, believable performances. Eric shared the duty of supervising the title character's animation with colleague Marc Davis. They both drew key personality scenes throughout the film, but it was Eric who was responsible for introducing Cinderella during the opening scenes. A few of her animal friends, including birds and mice, wake her up, and because she interacts with them in a playful, teasing way, Cinderella is instantly likeable. She sings "A Dream Is a Wish Your Heart Makes," which signals that she has not given up hope, even though her life has been reduced to the role of a kitchen maid. During the song she undoes her pigtails in a feminine and natural gesture.

Animating hair convincingly is not an easy thing to do. Unlike in computer animation, only a few pencil lines define its shape and movement. Eric enhanced the motion of Cinderella's hair by making it swing further, particularly during quick head turns. This overlapping action complements the character's principal movements in a natural way.

The film made after *Cinderella* presented a much younger heroine. But Alice from the movie *Alice in Wonderland* was also designed in a realistic way, and animators based their work on live-action reference. Eric was again asked to animate the title character's introductory scenes. Alice sits on a low branch of a tree listening to her sister, who reads from a history book. We understand instantly how bored Alice feels because she doesn't pay much attention. Instead she plays with a floral wreath,

Cinderella is instantly likeable in the opening scene.
© *Disney*

84

placing it on the head of her cat Dinah. These scenes are carefully drawn and help establish Alice as a real girl, who lives in her own colorful world. From a technical point of view, Alice's wide dress with its many folds presented something of an animation challenge. Every move she made needed to be complemented by the right kind of fold action. If not animated correctly, her dress would look too light or too heavy. But because Eric had earlier handled scenes with Cinderella and the Prince dancing, he already had a certain amount of experience moving folds on the fabric of a dress.

The trend to animate characters in opening sequences continued for Eric in the film *Peter Pan*. He drew scenes with Peter when we first see him at night on the rooftop of the Darling house. Kept in silhouette, his introduction is very effective, and Eric made him move like a dancer here. When a pose is held, it reads clearly. When Peter is in motion, it has a very fluid effect.

The animation for Alice was based on live-action reference.
© *Disney*

85

Peter Pan promises the Darling children a flight to Never Land.
© *Disney*

Milt Kahl handled the following scenes inside the nursery. Eric takes over when Peter teaches Wendy, John, and Michael how to fly. The technically complex animation required for the flight over London and on to Never Land is Eric's work as well. The children fly in perspective into camera and away from it while involved multiplane camera moves enhance their flight path.

Eric confessed later that this was hard work, but he was proud of the sequence because watching it gave you a thrill.

Milt Kahl helped Eric to keep Peter Pan on model by providing accurate key drawings for Eric's scenes. When Milt years later was asked by a reporter to comment on the film that followed, *Lady and the Tramp*, he said: "Well, the best thing in it is Eric's dog

Peg"—a high compliment from the studio's top draftsman. Eric himself always blushed a little when he related the fact that he based Peg's provocative moves after singer Peggy Lee, who voiced the character. The film features many great dog personalities, but Peg's performance is simply outstanding. Her character, with the past of a "worldly" showgirl, was a novelty in a Disney film, and Eric took full advantage of this new kind of material. During the song "He's a Tramp," Peg sings some of her lines over a raised shoulder with a Veronica Lake hairdo. She walks away from the camera and the spotlight as her tail and hip moves are greatly exaggerated.

Drawing, movement, timing, and appeal are perfect. Eric had become very comfortable animating all sorts of animals, and all that know-how helped turn Peg into an unexpected star of the film.

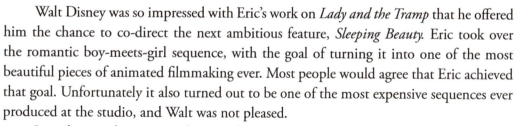

A beautiful rough animation drawing showing Peg in mid-song.
© Disney

Walt Disney was so impressed with Eric's work on *Lady and the Tramp* that he offered him the chance to co-direct the next ambitious feature, *Sleeping Beauty*. Eric took over the romantic boy-meets-girl sequence, with the goal of turning it into one of the most beautiful pieces of animated filmmaking ever. Most people would agree that Eric achieved that goal. Unfortunately it also turned out to be one of the most expensive sequences ever produced at the studio, and Walt was not pleased.

In order to achieve an enchanting forest setting for Aurora and Prince Phillip, Eric asked his layout and background artists to use the studio's multiplane camera extensively. Several individual painted layers of trees, bushes, and branches were photographed at various distances under the camera to create an illusion of real depth. Scenes like these were very effective in taking the audience into the world the characters are inhabiting, but they were also time-consuming and very costly to produce.

Eric went back into animation for the films that followed, *One Hundred and One Dalmatians*, *The Sword in the Stone*, *Mary Poppins*, and *The Jungle Book*. He didn't get the chance to develop any characters for these films in the way he had done in the past. His

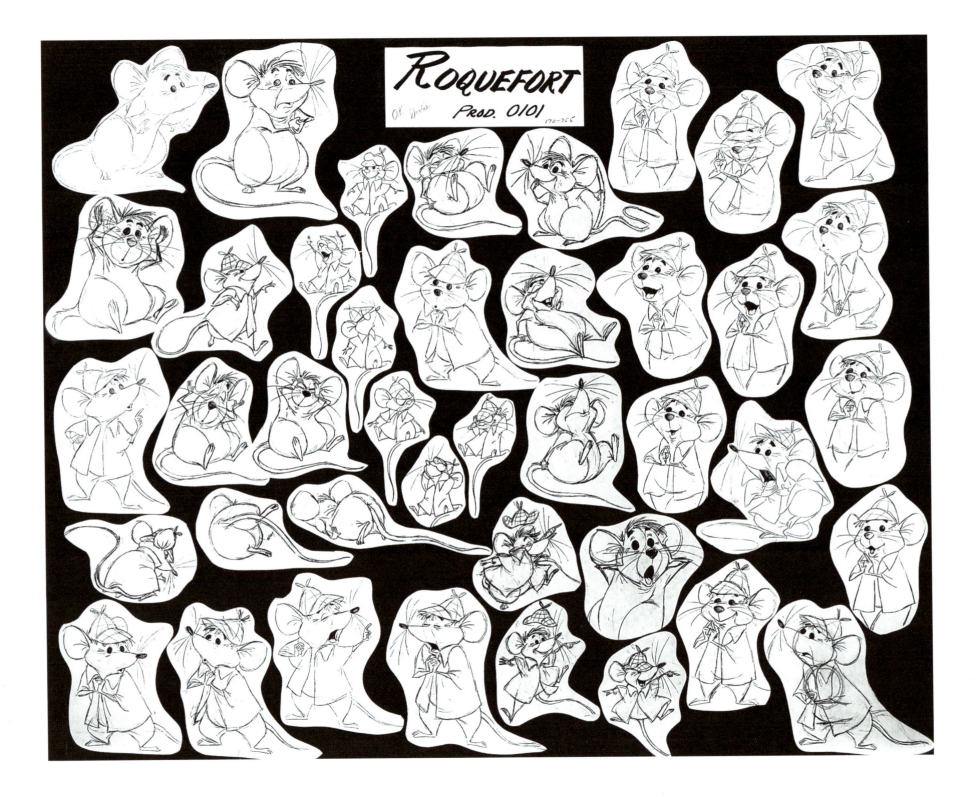

FACING PAGE
*Roquefort's model sheet,
made up of Eric's rough
animation drawings.*
© *Disney*

animation on the Dalmatian puppies, Sir Ector, Wart, Bagheera, and Mowgli is good, but lacks the charm and inventiveness of his earlier work. The final character Eric could call his own is the little mouse Roquefort in the film *The Aristocats*. Suddenly that Larson touch was back, and Eric turned this unusual assignment of a mouse who is friends with a family of cats into a most charming character.

Favorite scenes include Roquefort sharing a meal with Duchess and the kittens. He brings along a huge cracker, dips it in the cats' warm milk and munches away, making a lot of noise.

When he finds out that the cats have been kidnapped, he puts on a Sherlock Holmes costume and sets out to find them. Sterling Holloway voiced Roquefort beautifully, and Eric maintained quick mouse-like movements in the animation.

While work on *The Aristocats* continued, the studio started to realize that its animation department consisted mostly of artists who were getting near retirement age. It was decided that, in order to guarantee the future of Disney animation, new, young talent had to be found and trained in the classic techniques. Eric Larson turned out to be the perfect head of this new training program, which was structured in the following manner: Eric gave lectures on a regular basis on all topics regarding the production of Disney animation. He also worked with each trainee individually and helped them to express themselves in their animated scenes. Perfect motion was not good enough; character animation at Disney had to include the artist's individual point of view. Eric Larson's final contribution to the art of animation was enormous. He made sure that a new generation of animators saw the significance, the potential, and the challenge of Disney personality animation. Without his important involvement as a teacher and motivator, the film medium that Walt Disney had pioneered for many decades would have died in the 1970s.

The Three Caballeros

1945
THE FLYING GAUCHITO
GAUCHITO AND BURRITO
ROUGH ANIMATION
Sc. 37

During a bonding moment the Gauchito offers his winged donkey a sip of his *mate*, a South American drink. The Burrito jumps on the kid and both get entangled as they roll backwards. The final pose shows the donkey having a drink through a straw, the Gauchito beside him. To keep the action from looking complicated, Eric simplified the poses during the tumble. As the two characters straighten up, everything is back in place, including the *mate*. Throughout the scene, Eric defines the Burrito's anatomy very thoroughly.

After having worked on *Fantasia*'s flying horses, he was ready to apply that knowledge to a flying donkey, and make it look believable as well as entertaining.

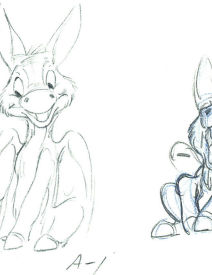

A-1

A-5

A-8

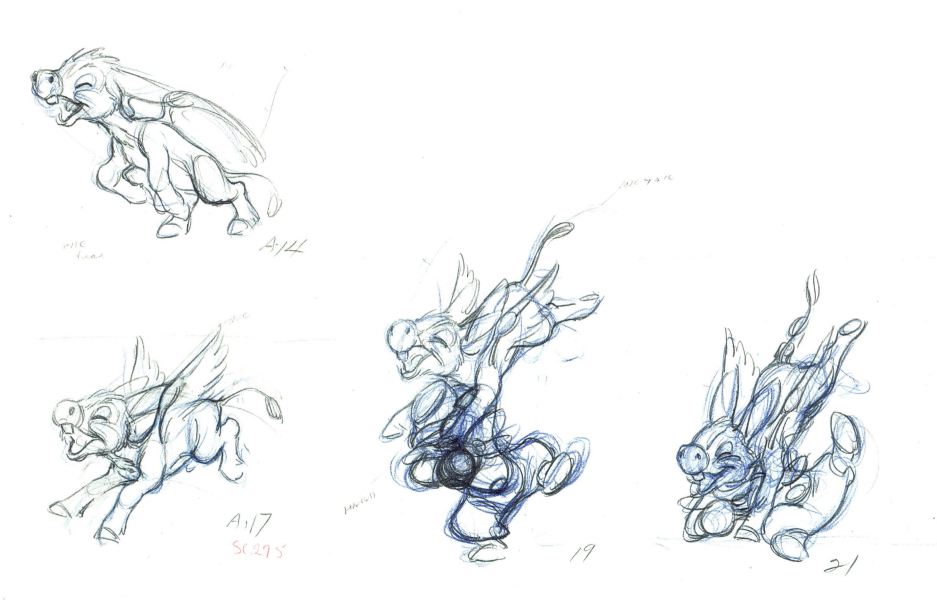

23

25

26

33

38

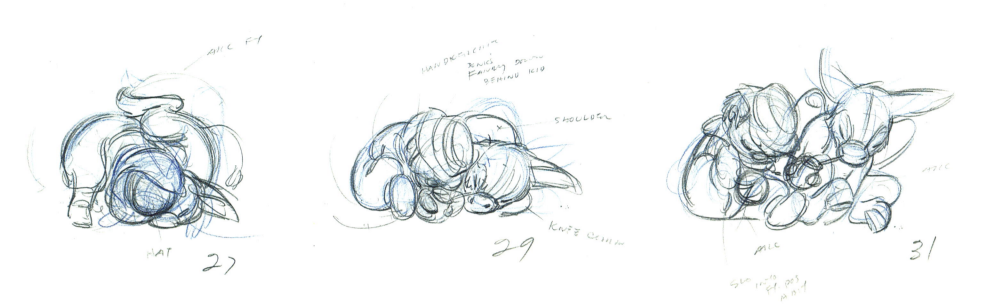

Peter Pan

1953
PETER PAN AND WENDY
CLEAN-UP ANIMATION
Seq. 2.1, Sc. 52

During a flying lesson, Peter Pan tries his best to get Wendy airborne. Not until the third try does Wendy take to the air. In itself this is a powerful statement regarding animated characters. Just as in real life, things often don't work the first time around, it takes repeated efforts. This scene would feel very boring if Peter had succeeded the first time around. But by failing a couple of times, a sincere human touch is added to what otherwise would have been just an ordinary continuity scene without much personality.

On a technical level, the overlapping motion on Wendy's loose skirt helps to give the scene a beautiful flow and rhythm.

© Disney

94

89

92

94

97

$\mathcal{L}$ady and the $\mathcal{T}$ramp

1955
PEG
ROUGH ANIMATION
Seq. 10, Sc. 81

During the dog pound sequence, Peg struts toward the back of the cell, singing: "And I wish that I could travel his way… wish that I could travel his way…"

Eric famously studied singer Peggy Lee's walk and applied her sashaying quality to this dog character, whose personality is somewhat seductive. He exaggerated the hip movement from left to right, each time one rear leg contacts the ground. Since Lee emphasized the word "way" several times during her song, Eric flairs out Peg's tail in order to visually accentuate these beats. This is a beautiful character walk for a dog with a showgirl past.

© Disney

51

55

69

118

158

163

185

190

209

218

18

221

*O*ne *H*undred and *O*ne *D*almatians

1961
ROLLY
CLEAN-UP ANIMATION
Seq. 15, Sc. 46

After the cows in the barn generously offer their milk to the starving Dalmatian puppies, Rolly tries desperately to get close to one of the udders. After a few failed attempts he manages to climb on to a stool. By leaning forward and balancing himself on Lucky's head he almost succeeds. But instead his weight drags him down and he falls on his belly—still no milk. Eric wanted to show that Rolly is a little clumsy, so on his way to the top of the stool, his right rear foot slips, but he manages in the end. Little mishaps like this help to create a character whose efforts aren't always perfect. It gives this scene texture, but also more interest, because a little Dalmatian who struggles is more enjoyable to watch than one who just goes through the motion flawlessly.

© *Disney*

© Disney

101

102

107

126

130

135

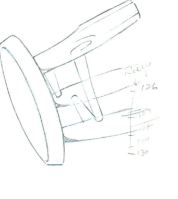

The Sword in the Stone

1963
MADAME MIM AS DRAGON
CLEAN-UP ANIMATION
Seq. 10, Sc. 144

The duel of the wizards is over, and Madam Mim has lost the battle. Against all rules, she had turned herself into a dragon, but Merlin outsmarted her by becoming a germ and Mim caught the disease. To show her frustration, Eric animated a childlike temper tantrum. "Oh… you sneaky old scoundrel!" Mim pulls on her purple hair, and bounces up and down, which makes the ground tremble. At the end she resigns exhaustedly and leans back against a tree. Eric drew extreme, but funny expressions throughout the scene to show Mim's fury. As her upper body moves backward, the legs come up for counterbalance, which results in a hilarious final pose.

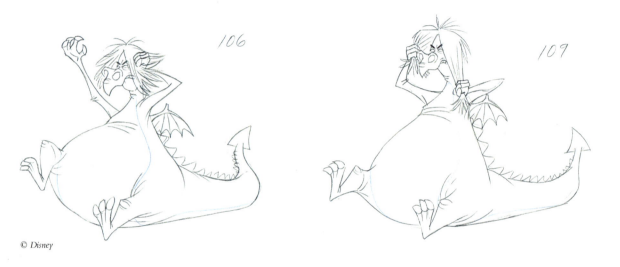

© Disney

112

113

115

© Disney

117

122

130

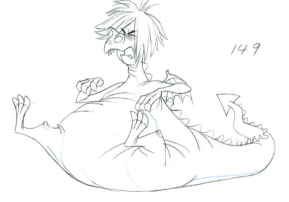

144

146

149

133

136

141

156

Ward Kimball

Early in 1937, Ward Kimball was not happy about working for Walt Disney. As a matter of fact he was seriously thinking about quitting the studio. *Snow White and the Seven Dwarfs* was in the final phase of production, and every artist involved with the film was working enthusiastically and long hours to meet deadlines. Yet Kimball could not share the crew's sentiment, he was brooding. Practically all of his animation had just been cut out of the movie.

He was told that his sequence involving the seven dwarfs eating soup proved irrelevant to the film's plot line. Another animated section that showed the dwarfs building a bed for Snow White had been eliminated as well for the same reason. Ward had contributed scenes for this piece as well. What remained of his work were a few shots with the vultures, as they fly above the Witch, who is making her way into the forest toward the dwarfs' cottage. A meeting with Ward and Disney was scheduled, and its outcome could have been the end of Kimball's career at the studio.

What happened instead proved that Walt Disney was a master when it came to dealing with any of his artists' problems. Ward left that meeting anxious to get back to his drawing board. Walt had just given him a brand new assignment, a character who would play an important role in the studio's next animated feature *Pinocchio*. Kimball was going to develop and animate Jiminy Cricket, and he was promoted to supervising animator. Disney's passion as well as his powers of persuasion had just helped him to avoid losing one of his most important artists. Kimball's subsequent career at the studio was long and fruitful, but not without the occasional bump in the road.

Ward Kimball was hired on April 2, 1934. He was placed into the in-betweener pool, which included a group of newcomers who learned the ropes by assisting experienced animators. After helping out on short films like *The Wise Little Hen* and *The Goddess of Spring*, he was finally given the chance to do some of his own animation on the short *Elmer Elephant*. Ward impressed senior animator Ham Luske with his first attempts as a solo animator. This led to an assignment that catered to Kimball's musical talents. In the short *Woodland Café* he animated several jazz musicians portrayed by insects. The energy of the jazzy musical track is perfectly captured in the fast-timed animation. Ward's own enthusiasm as a musician comes through in the insects' exuberant, rubber-hose

THE NINE OLD MEN : *Ward Kimball*

movements. The feet are tapping, hands work themselves in and out of camera, and the whole body reacts to the musical rhythm. These scenes caught the attention of many people at the studio, and perhaps later gave Walt Disney the idea to have Ward develop a certain insect for the film *Pinocchio*.

Spirited, perfectly timed musical moves signal Kimball's attitude toward his work. Pure fun.
© Disney

113

The looseness showcased in Kimball's early animation was much more suitable to cartoony characters than realistic ones. When the studio began work on *Snow White*, it was no surprise that Ward ended up in the dwarfs unit. His main sequence might have been cut from the film but looking at individual drawings from this deleted section, we can only marvel at the way Ward exaggerated the dwarfs' faces without ever losing the characters' charm.

When these scenes were deleted from Snow White, *Ward very nearly quit working for Walt Disney.*
© Disney

114

Charm was a quality Ward had a very hard time getting into his next assignment—Jiminy Cricket from the film *Pinocchio*. "A cricket looks like a cross between a cockroach and a grasshopper," he stated in a later interview. Naturally, as a Disney artist, it is obvious to start researching the characteristics of the real insect. But each time Ward would show Walt Disney an updated design of Jiminy for approval, the boss' response was always the same: too ugly, lacks appeal. After more frustrating attempts and virtually eliminating any resemblance to a real cricket he finally succeeded in getting Walt's OK. By this time Jiminy looked appealing, but not much like an insect at all. Instead his proportions were similar to Mickey Mouse's.

SUGGESTIONS FOR CRICKET
IN
• SEQ. 1, 1-1, 1-5
PINOCCHIO
F-3

CHARACTER MODEL DEP'T.
O.K. by **JG** DATE **2-6-39**
NUMBER **M-175-A**
MODEL SHEETS SUBJECT TO CHANGE
WITHOUT NOTICE
© Walt Disney Enterprises

2003

Early designs based on real crickets and
(opposite) Kimball's final version of Jiminy.
© Disney

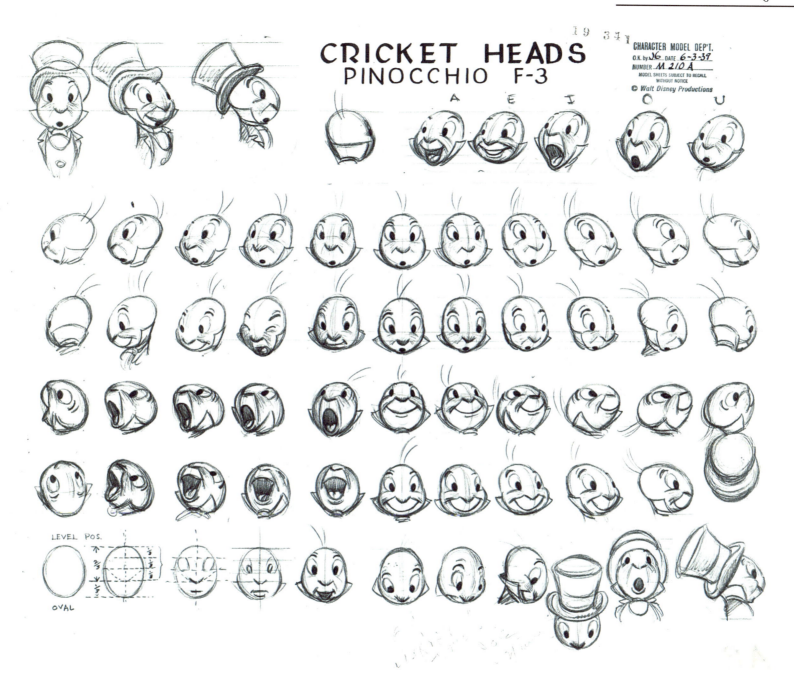

CRICKET HEADS
PINOCCHIO F-3

CHARACTER MODEL DEP'T.
O.K. by J6 DATE 6-3-39
NUMBER M 210 A
MODEL SHEETS SUBJECT TO RECALL
WITHOUT NOTICE
© Walt Disney Productions

117

Ward might not have been entirely happy with Jiminy Cricket's appearance, but he most certainly succeeded in developing his personality as a caring and likable mentor to Pinocchio. He might look like a little man without ears, but he jumps high like a real cricket. The timing in his acting is quick and contrasting, but the overall performance is always sincere and believable. The audience likes Jiminy instantly, because he cares so much about Pinocchio. Just like Mickey Mouse, his poses are strong and easy to read. Occasionally Ward gave him complex dance moves that are a joy to watch. After Pinocchio comes to life with the help of the Blue Fairy, they both celebrate while singing "Give a Little Whistle." Again Ward's musicality comes forward during Jiminy's line: "And always let your conscience be your guide." The dance steps are incredibly complicated when analyzed; every body part is doing something differently, yet the whole works in rhythmic perfection. Complex scenes like these require 24 drawings per second (simple and slow-moving scenes usually involve only 12). Here every single drawing is all-important and needs to be made by the animator. There aren't any in-betweens that could be passed on to the assistant.

Few Disney feature characters achieve top stardom like Jiminy Cricket. Once audiences have embraced such a personality, they are eager to see more appearances. Jiminy and Tinker Bell from *Peter Pan* both have become icons who represent not only The Walt Disney Studios, but animation as a whole. These ambassadors introduce TV shows, they are main attractions in theme parks and have become popular merchandise characters. In other words their popularity has afforded them an afterlife. Kimball's next animated character required again careful synchronization between movement and music. Bacchus from the "Pastoral" sequence in *Fantasia* and his donkey-unicorn Jacchus are an unequal pair. The little mule has a hard time carrying the oversized god of wine, but his off-balance moves presented possibilities for funny character animation. Bacchus is interested in only two things, wine and the alluring "centaurettes." A chubby and intoxicated personality like him moves in unsteady and wobbly ways, which are all synced here to the beat of Beethoven's music. Even though there are some fun moments to animate, particularly during the dance, Ward was not very fond of this assignment. The character's design as well as his role in the film didn't come up to his standards. He enviously watched his colleagues who pulled out all the stops when animating the hilarious parody of the ballet "Dance of the Hours". "Once in a while something perfect comes along," Ward stated years later. "The 'Dance of the Hours' turned out as perfect as it gets."

Bacchus and Jacchus might not have been favorite assignments, but Ward still managed to animate them with comic gusto.
© Disney

119

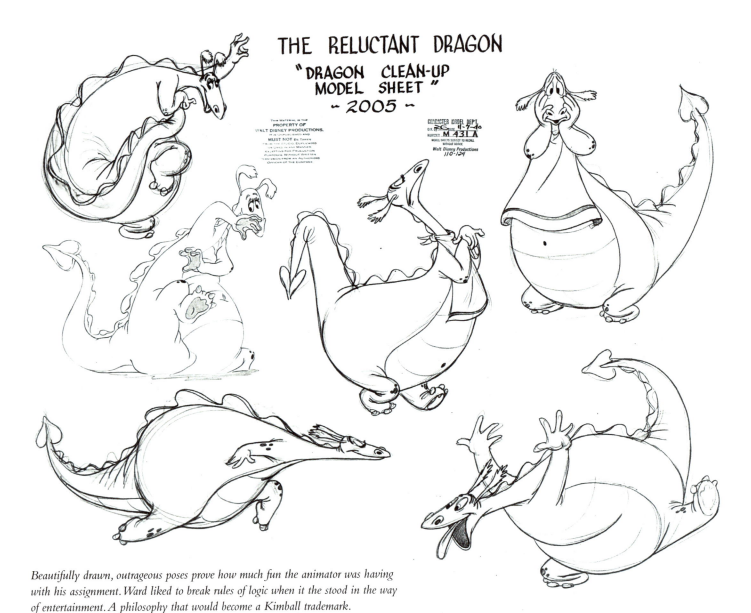

THE RELUCTANT DRAGON
"DRAGON CLEAN-UP
MODEL SHEET"
~ 2005 ~

CHARACTER MODEL DEPT.
O.K. BY _____ DATE 4-7-40
NUMBER M.431 A
MODEL SHEETS SUBJECT TO RECALL
WITHOUT NOTICE
Walt Disney Productions
110-124

*Beautifully drawn, outrageous poses prove how much fun the animator was having
with his assignment. Ward liked to break rules of logic when it the stood in the way
of entertainment. A philosophy that would become a Kimball trademark.*
© Disney

In the film *The Reluctant Dragon*, Ward finally found a role that offered a tour de force acting opportunity: a cartoony looking dragon who is expected to put up a fight with local knights.

But instead the Dragon is petrified at the mere thought of a combat—it turns out he is a poet who enjoys his afternoon tea. Actor Barnett Parker's voice suggested a flamboyant type who would express himself through theatrical gestures. Ward charged at this rich material and created one of his all-time great animated personalities. His acting choices are perfectly in line with the dialogue recordings: flamboyant acting at its best. At one point the Dragon invites the Boy to a picnic on his belly. He decides to recite a poem he wrote about an upside-down cake. He so sympathizes with the cake's dilemma because its top is on the bottom, he is even moved to tears and gives it a little kiss. It is absolutely hilarious to see how sincere the dragon is during his performance. Kimball's poses communicate a character who is acting in front of an audience. A few years ago Ward was reminiscing about the character and said that the Reluctant Dragon was probably the first gay character in the history of animation.

By now Kimball's expressive and inventive style of animation was recognized and admired by most of his co-workers. It came as no surprise that Ward would not join the *Bambi* unit, instead he was offered to develop a group of crows for the film *Dumbo*. These birds played a crucial part in the story. They first ridicule Dumbo after being told that he had flown into a tree. Eventually they become convinced and try everything they can to make Dumbo take to the sky again.

Ward particularly enjoyed animating their song number "When I See an Elephant Fly." He managed to create five different crow personalities with Jim Crow as the boss. Everybody moves according to their body type—skinny, tall, or chubby, etc. As they walk and strut, singing along, the timing is punchy and fluid at the same time. Jim Crow at one point rotates one of his legs completely illogically, anatomically speaking, before kicking it out. Two other crows lean against each other dancing away from the camera, except their combined silhouette only shows two legs instead of four. Breaking the rules of logic in order to present something unexpected is a quality Kimball relished. Some directors and animators at the studio questioned this approach, thinking that believability is being lost with this kind of surreal animation. But Ward remained undeterred, this was the way he saw the medium of animation, an ongoing experiment in how to entertain in new ways.

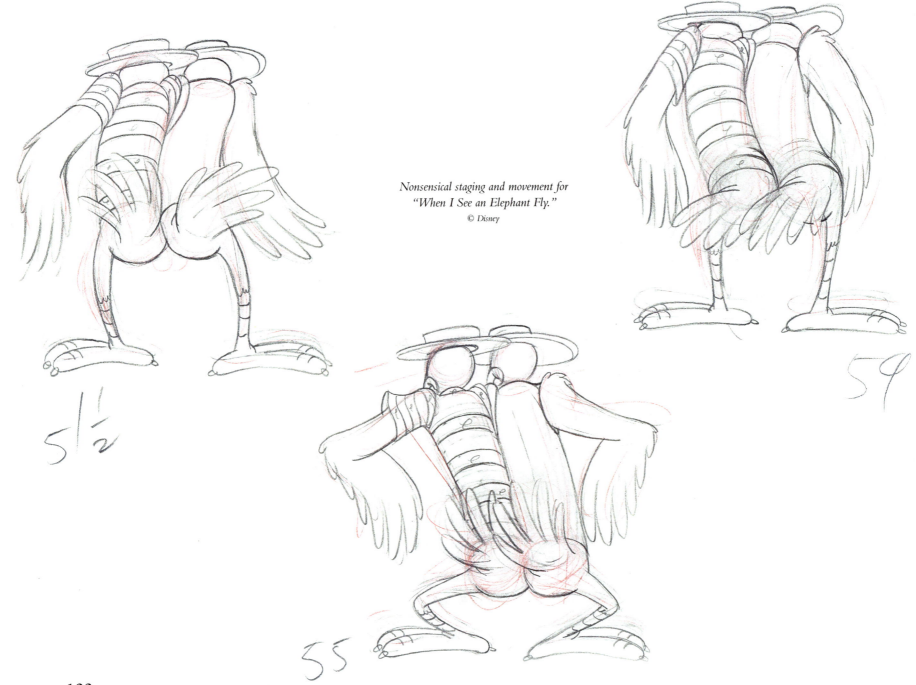

Nonsensical staging and movement for
"When I See an Elephant Fly."
© *Disney*

During the early 1940s Ward brought his unconventional sensibilities to Disney short films as well. For the Mickey Mouse short *The Nifty Nineties*, Ward got to animate a very unusual sequence, one that involved two characters who turned out to be caricatures of Disney animators.

The first one was Ward himself, the second one was his friend, animator Fred Moore. The walls of Kimball's office had long been filled with gag drawings depicting these two in mischievous situations, so it didn't seem far-fetched to utilize their designs as animated vaudeville performers for an audience that included Mickey and Minnie Mouse. They tap dance across the stage, then pause for a moment, so Ward can tell Fred a joke: "Hey brown eyes, who is that lady I saw you with last night?" "That was no lady, that was my wife!" Laughter follows, and Ward hits Fred on the head with a hammer. This is slapstick cartoon business, and Kimball tried everything to present it in a funny ways. On Fred's last dialogue line, the word wife is animated by suddenly enlarging his mouth disproportionally. This is an odd choice, but because it comes unexpectedly it looks very funny. Ward proves again that you can't go wrong by surprising the audience.

Fred Moore as silly vaudeville entertainer.
© Disney

More juicy animation assignments kept coming Ward's way. The 1945 film *The Three Caballeros* featured a big song number with Donald Duck, Panchito Pistoles, and José Carioca. Kimball, who animated the whole musical number, explained his approach for the animation during a 1984 interview:

> I was given this long song that went on for three or four minutes with no business. So I listened to the song for about a week. I turned all the lights off in the room and just listened to the song, visualizing it. I said there is nothing I can do except being literal about it. When they say: "We're three happy chappies with snappy serapes," all of a sudden the serapes appear. One of the first criticisms, when the director saw the pencil test, was: The duck goes out on the right, and he comes in on the left. And the rooster goes out on the top, and he comes in from the bottom. You can't do that, it's not logical. You have to have these tie ups, you have to make sense. And I said: Look, who cares? A guy runs out on the left and comes in on the right. I mean, that gives it its flavor, its craziness.

Luckily when Walt saw the sequence, he had no objections whatsoever. And the song's animation remained intact.

Ward turned the song number in The Three Caballeros *into one of animation's most hilarious and surreal moments.*
© *Disney*

Walt Disney knew by now about Ward's strength as an animator who, with each assignment, strived for new ways of doing things. Kimball himself stated once that animation requires an endless amount of drawings, so why repeat yourself when there is a chance to do something in a different way? As wacky as some of his scenes might have turned out, they still have a believable quality because Ward was an excellent draftsman who animated his characters with real weight. Without weight there is only graphic movement, which involves an audience only to a point. But by moving different parts of the body separately and timing them based on what they are made of (body mass, hair, clothing) the animated whole will come to life. Ward applied these rules in everything he did, and his assignment to animate several characters for the short *Peter and the Wolf* was no exception. He drew key scenes with the Sasha the cat and Sonia the duck.

But his most inventive and original animation can be seen when the three hunters arrive. Mischa, Yascha, and Vladimir are entirely comical characters. As huners they look about as effective as the Three Stooges. When the little bird Sasha tries to get their attention to inform them about Peter's plight, the befuddled and confused troop runs around in circles before regrouping.

Kimball's way of moving these characters is nothing short of breathtaking. As they make their way through the forest, the leg movements range from tip-toeing to long strides. When they find out about the danger ahead, they charge forward, propelled by unrealistic circular leg motion.

Ward squeezes every bit of fun out of this trio, which includes constant bouncing of their hats as well as loose follow-through action in their clothing.

It is obvious that Kimball relished bringing these clumsy hunters to life.

© Disney

125

Ward's next character assignment would be comical again, but a little more skilled and accomplished than the three Russian hunters. *Pecos Bill* is part of the 1948 full-length feature *Melody Time*. The character was primarily animated by Ward Kimball and Milt Kahl, two highly skilled animators with somewhat different ideologies. Kahl insisted on masterfully drawn animation that showed natural, believable movement. Kimball on the other hand was driven by a need to experiment and invent in order to maximize the entertainment. Astonishingly *Pecos Bill* works seamlessly in continuity, there is only one version of the character on the screen. Ward animated the opening scenes when young Pecos falls off a moving wagon. He is left behind and eventually raised by coyotes. He befriends an infant horse, later named Widowmaker. As adults we see the two of them bonding during outrageous adventures like chasing a cyclone as well as roping and pulling a raincloud from California all the way to Texas for drought relief. All this outrageous story material was perfectly suited for Kimball, who always preferred working with such impossible situations. He even animated a scene with Pecos and Widowmaker yodeling into the camera as they are riding along. In order to show the mouth actions clearly Ward underplayed the overall body movement, so the viewer remains focused on the expressive yodeling phrasing.

From a technical point of view, these scenes were very involved. The horse on one hand is running, jumping and rearing up, while Pecos on top is lassoing, shooting, and singing. The action analysis alone might have been too difficult for many animators, but Kimball made it look easy.

After animating scenes for both sections of the film *The Adventures of Ichabod and Mr. Toad*, Ward joined the team that would re-establish the Disney full-length animated feature film with *Cinderella*. He was put in charge to develop the stepmother's evil cat Lucifer, who often interacted with a sympathetic group of resident mice. At the time Ward was criticized for his design of Lucifer, as a cartoony, fat villain with almost no believable anatomy. The human cast was animated with the help of life-action reference, and their animation required careful drawing combined with realistic motion, in stark contrast to Lucifer. But Kimball didn't care, this was the way he was going to approach the cat. And Walt Disney did not object, because he might have foreseen the type of entertainment Ward would come up with for the cat and mice. One sequence in particular turned out to be a comedic

HORSE and BILL model *Pecos Bill*

Prod. 2056

A model sheet made up from Kimball's key animation poses.
© Disney

Kimball's model sheet of Lucifer reveals strong poses and evil expressions, in spite of an overall cartoony appearance.

© Disney

128

masterpiece. As Cinderella arranges breakfast items on trays for her stepfamily members, Lucifer frantically searches for the mouse Gus under the cups.

This is a fight against time, because soon the trays will be taken upstairs. Lucifer's paranoid timing accelerates, because he knows the mouse is somewhere under one of the cups. The fact that the audience knows at all times where Gus is hiding just adds to this hilarious pantomime scene. Even animation maestro Milt Kahl admitted years later: "I could never have done anything like that."

Ward again avoided getting cast on a realistic character when production began for *Alice in Wonderland*. This time he was given the opportunity to animate a whole range of eccentric personalities. Although some of them were human characters, they did not conform to the world Alice came from. After all, this was Wonderland. Tweedledum and Tweedledee move as if their bodies were water balloons. They constantly bounce into each other as they introduce themselves. Actually Ward uses this physical contact to great comical effect. The eccentric animation is perfectly timed to lively music and silly sound effects. As so often before, Kimball enjoys inventing unusual leg movements that go against any logic. He breaks the knees in order to get a wacky effect, anything to make them move in unrealistic but entertaining ways.

Tweedledum and Tweedledee move as if their bodies were water balloons.
© Disney

129

What made the Mad Tea Party so outstanding was the fact that absolutely nothing made sense, yet poor Alice tries repeatedly to reason with crazy characters like the Mad Hatter and the March Hare. Although some live action was filmed, Kimball's animation shows no trace of any such reference. He did pick up pieces of business from actors Ed Wynn and Jerry Colonna, but by incorporating this into his broad animation, the results look original and fresh. This kind of lively, cartoony animation can easily look overactive when not timed properly. In all of this frisky movement there needed to be moments of pause in order to show the characters thinking, otherwise any personality statement gets lost in hectic graphic motion. Ward of course knew this very well. He would take advantage of these quieter intervals and add funny but subtle bits of action like an ear wiggle or unusual dialogue shapes.

The Mad Hatter's tongue was used to animate his dialogue with a lisp.
© *Disney*

The equally mad March Hare.
© *Disney*

130

The Cheshire Cat was animated in an entirely different way. Ward underplayed this character to bring out his schizophrenic personality. Different parts of the cat's body appear and disappear slowly, and his smooth movements are peculiar and offbeat. He can literally remove his head and stand on it. He also gestures with his hind legs. Kimball considered the Cheshire Cat to be the real mad one in the film.

The psychotic Cheshire Cat might move slowly, but he expresses pure insanity.
© Disney

131

There was not nearly as much madness to be found in Disney's next animated feature, *Peter Pan*. The title character as well as the children were conceived as being real flesh and blood characters, not the kind of assignment Ward would look forward to getting involved with. Around this time, several of the other animators voiced their disapproval of not ever getting the type of juicy assignments that Ward had enjoyed over the years. Marc Davis stated that he and Milt Kahl most of the time ended up animating the realistic human characters, while Kimball had all the fun doing cartoony stuff. Nevertheless, Walt Disney knew his animators' strengths (and weaknesses) very well, and he cast Ward on the Indian Chief. Needless to say this imposing, authoritative character turned out to be as entertaining as anything Ward had done in the past. In most of the Chief's scenes he acts very serious and stern, not very compelling qualities. What Ward focused on, in order to get humor into the animation, was the way the Indian Chief talked. His large mouth configuration is somewhat unique with a long upper lip and deep wrinkles. Unique mouth shapes and punchy timing give great interest to his dialogue scenes. It's just fun to see him say the name of his daughter Tiger Lily and watch his tongue wiggle inside his mouth.

Unusual dialogue animation helped to enrich the Indian Chief's personality.
© *Disney*

132

Modern graphics help alter the conventional Disney style.
© *Disney*

When work began on *Lady and the Tramp*, Ward realized that the trend toward realism in Disney features meant fewer opportunities to express himself. Perhaps the two villainous cats Si and Am could be handled in a way that would be in line with his artistic sensibilities. Kimball went all out to make them vicious, zany, and unpredictable. Unfortunately the results did not fit in with the overall styling of the film, and Ward was taken off the picture. He subsequently took on the job of director/animator for the experimental musical short film *Toot, Whistle, Plunk and Boom*, which presented the history of musical instruments throughout the world. Back in his element, Ward pushed the boundaries of Disney animation, this time on a smaller budget. Limited animation had been pioneered before at other animation studios like UPA, and Ward was fascinated by the challenge of finding entertainment with minimal motion on the screen. Very often the character's body is held in one drawing, while only a hand or an eye moves. The overall visual statement can be much more poignant than what full, all-involved character animation offers. Traditional Disney characters become living, breathing beings, but in limited animation the motion is greatly reduced, and the viewer accepts that flat drawings communicate a more restrained kind of acting.

The film Mars and Beyond *explored the possibilities of alien life forms.*
© *Disney*

Ward once again did not fit in with the studio's next animated feature *Sleeping Beauty*, where the focus was on stylized but realistic drawing and serious storytelling. Luckily other opportunities came along when Disney entered the world of television. A series of shows dealing with man's future in outer space was being developed, and Kimball was put in charge as a director. Limited animation was again used to achieve dramatic as well as comical results. These TV shows were hugely successful, and Ward later recalled that this period at the studio might have been his happiest.

After such a creative and innovative chapter as a director at the studio, Ward all of a sudden found himself at odds with his boss, Walt Disney, while he was supervising sequences on the mostly live-action film *Babes in Toyland*. Walt was unhappy with Ward's story work as well as the choices he made for casting actors. In heavy disagreement, Ward found himself "demoted" back to animator. In the early 1960s he was put to work on TV shows featuring the new character Ludwig Von Drake. Kimball animated several entertaining sequences, but the old Kimball animated spark was missing. Nevertheless, after Walt's death in 1966, Ward still experienced a couple of career high points. He directed the Academy Award-winning animated/live action short *It's Tough to Be a Bird*, and in 1971 he served as animation director for the mostly live-action film *Bedknobs and Broomsticks*. The movie's highlight is a soccer game played by various animated animals on the island of Naboombu. Here the Kimball touch is evident in almost every scene, as the anthropomorphic characters play the game by making use of their animal characteristics. The goalkeeper elephant shoots the ball across the field with his trunk, while the cheetah runs so fast that his feet catch on fire. This is a hilarious sequence that only reaches comedic highs because of Ward's involvement. It turned out to be his last contribution to Disney animation before he retired in 1973.

Ward Kimball's long career as a Disney animator and director is unique; no one else put that much effort into expanding the horizon of character animation. With each assignment he kept asking himself: What can I do differently this time around? His hyper experimental spirit was always grounded in superb classic draftsmanship and in a great sense for original comedy. No matter how off-the-wall his characters might behave, they always came across as believable and enjoyable. Today's animation community can still benefit and learn from Ward's rich body of work, as well as his philosophy: why repeat yourself when there is a chance to do something different?

Ferdinand the Bull

1938
PICADOR ON HORSE
ROUGH ANIMATION
Sc. 39

Ahead of Ferdinand's planned bullfight, a line of various fighters parade into the arena before the matador. Kimball animated all of these characters. Their designs represent caricatures of Disney animators, and this picador on a dilapidated horse is star animator Bill Tytla. The fact that Ward placed him on such a battered horse shows that he is poking fun at his highly regarded colleague. The Tytla character moves ever so proudly up and down from the saddle, exuding an almost ridiculous amount of confidence.

The horse is animated by walking in place in accordance with the camera move. The feet seem to slide on the ground but, combined with the moving background, the connection between character and scenery is perfect. This method of working out a piece of action during a camera move was preferred by most animators. Using an alternate way of handling a scene like this, one would be animating the character physically across the page, and then on to another one. By staying in place would seem like a simpler way of doing this, but it required precise synchronization with the increments of the camera move.

These few drawings only represent a small portion of this long and labor-intense multi-character scene.

© Disney

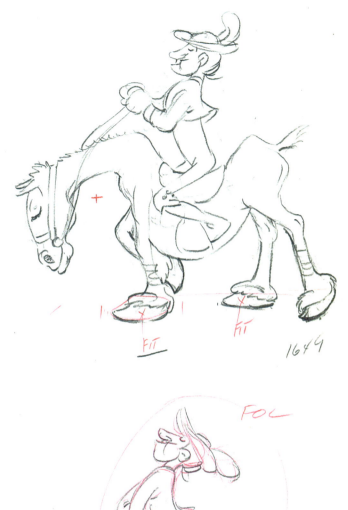

Fantasia

1940
BACCHUS
ROUGH ANIMATION
Seq. 4.3, Sc. 43

It is astonishing to see how rough Ward Kimball's drawings for this scene are. And yet, he keeps control of this chubby god of wine throughout the broad animation, which is carefully timed to the music of Beethoven. Bacchus is chasing and interacting with various centaurettes. His body mass is treated like a water balloon that spins out of control at the end of the scene. The counter-movement of the long, soft cape adds to the overall fluid feel to the scene.

On some of the drawings Kimball indicated lightly key positions for centaurettes, which were later handled by animator Jack Bradbury.

© Disney

138

139

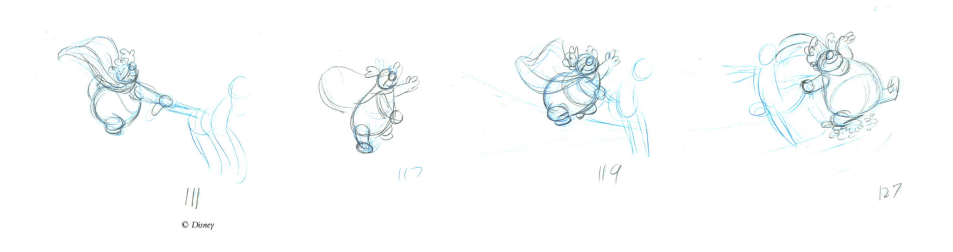

Make Mine Music / Peter and the Wolf

1946
HUNTERS
ROUGH ANIMATION
Seq. 7, Sc. 99

These few rough drawings show two of the three hunters being startled by Peter's whistle sound coming from up high in a tree. They had all been informed of the boy's encounter with the dangerous wolf, and their reaction is portrayed as a wild, nervous scramble of movements before running into each other.

Extremely broad action like this is played for comedy and paints the hunters as relatively harmless and confused characters.

This is a textbook example of two cartoony body masses smashing together, then separating before falling to the ground.

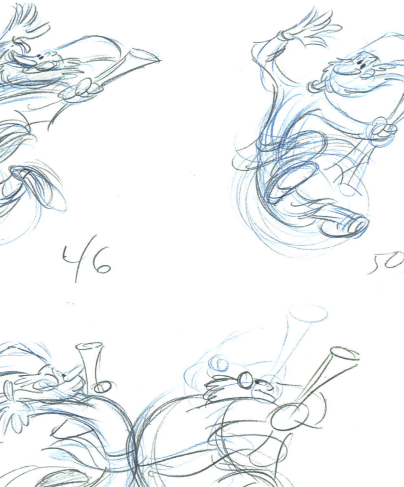

© Disney

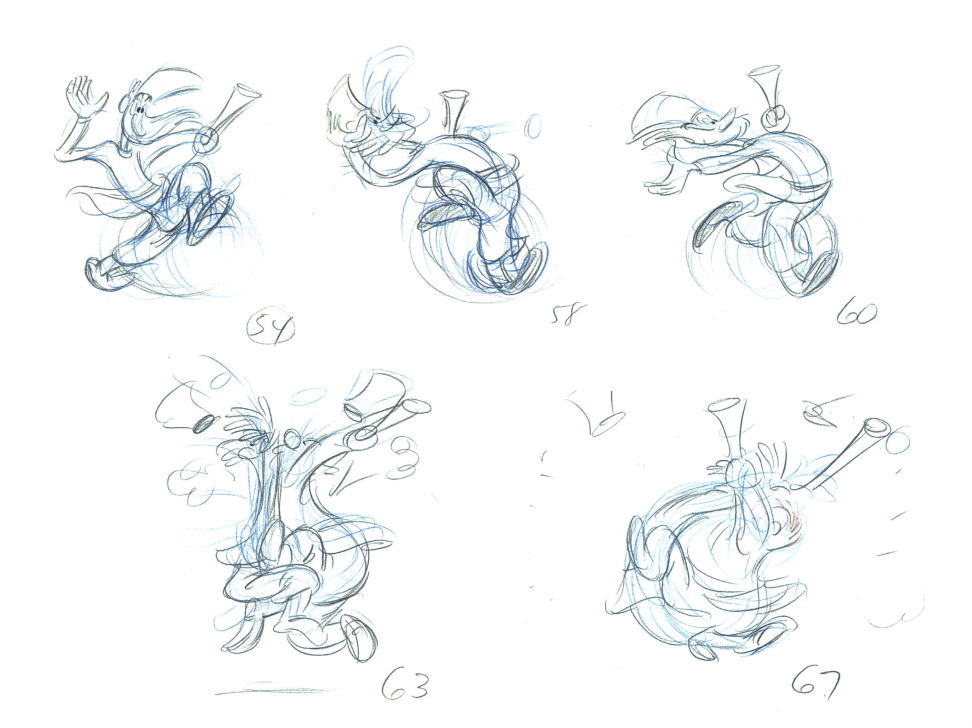

Cinderella

1950
LUCIFER
CLEAN-UP ANIMATION
Seq. 1.6, Sc. 63

In an effort to portray Lucifer not only as evil, but also as an eerie and bizarre character, Kimball invented this sneaky motion as the cat follows Cinderella up the stairs. At this moment his attention is on a mouse which is hiding under one of the tea cups placed on the tray Cinderella is carrying. This quick feline movement is completely illogical, as Lucifer's body stays low to the ground and conforms to the shape of the steps, creating a zigzag move. There is a confident, but also deviant quality to the scene. Lucifer believes that if he stays determined in his pursuit, it will only be a matter of time before that mouse becomes a snack.

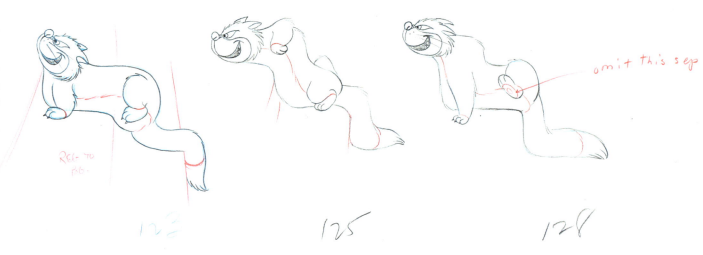

144

REG TO BG.

115

REG TO BG

117

118

RBG.

120

131

133

RBG TO BG.

136

Alice in Wonderland

1951
TWEEDLEDUM
CLEAN-UP ANIMATION
Seq. 5, Sc. 36

In this scene Tweedledum leaves his buddy Tweedledee offscreen as he starts to recite the story of the Walrus and the Carpenter to a curious Alice.

He sings with a characteristic lisp: "The thun watch shining on the thea, shining with all hith might…" During the line, Kimball moves Tweedledum to the right and then to the left. The body action can be broken up into three segments.

The upper body is involved in various arm gestures, the round belly squashes and stretches slowly throughout, and the legs perform illogical twirling moves. Everything works well together with entertaining results. This unrealistic approach to movement places this character firmly in the surreal world of Wonderland.

© Disney

146

147

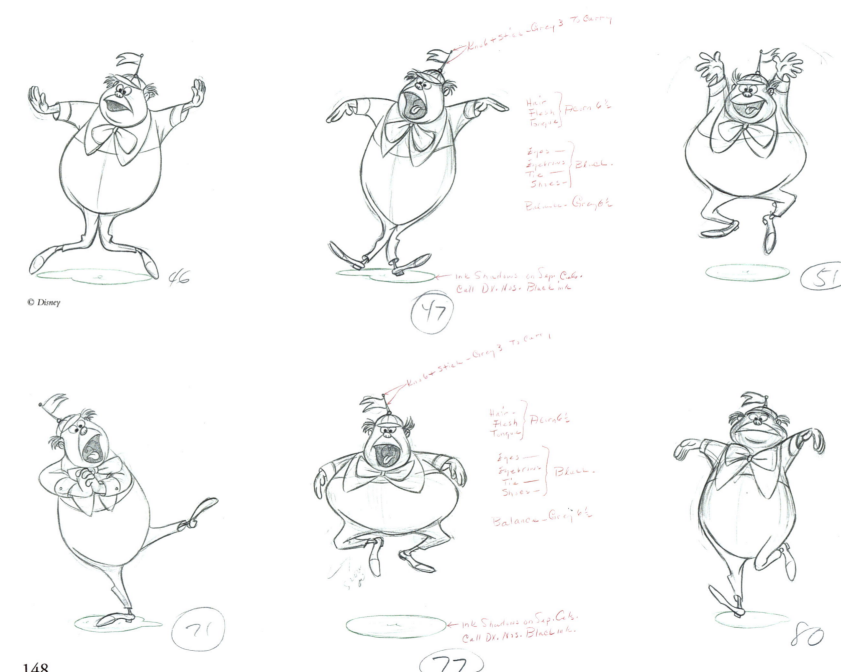

148

53

59

63

67

82

86

91

TO ART
VERY BEST REGARDS,
Milt
30.4.76

Milt Kahl

Animator Milt Kahl wasn't happy with the way the character of Pinocchio was coming along in late 1937. During a meeting he voiced his disapproval; the design just did not look appealing to him.

He received a certain look from other artists in the room, then one of the directors, feeling somewhat annoyed, asked Milt to put his pencil where his mouth was.

So the 28-year-old animator went to work, trying to prove that he was perfectly able to improve on the existing design of Pinocchio. Milt's approach went in a new direction, his drawings showed the character as a charming little boy, who just happened to have joints like a marionette. The fact that he was made out of wood was of secondary importance.

It turned out that Walt Disney just loved Milt's new designs, and subsequently promoted him to supervising animator for Pinocchio. Eventually Ollie Johnston and Frank Thomas joined the unit that would be responsible for animating important personality sequences with the title character.

Early design concepts and Kahl's improved look for the character.
© Disney

152

Starting with Pinocchio, Walt relied more and more on Milt Kahl's extraordinary draftsmanship and his sense for designing characters.

Ollie Johnston stated years later that Milt's drawings always stood out and showed the personalities in a very believable way. He added: "I've been called crazy, but I do believe that Milt draws as well as Michelangelo."

Walt Disney was very lucky to have a master draftsman on staff, and Milt Kahl was fortunate to join his studio at a time when his special talents thoroughly lent themselves to the demands of this new art form. "I turned out to be just perfect for this medium," Milt pronounced confidently during an interview in the early 1980s. Earlier he told assistant Dave Michener: "I'm the best draftsman around here—that's not bragging, that's a fact!"

Even before the production of *Pinocchio*, Milt had made a name for himself as a class animator. His work on short films like *Ferdinand, the Bull* and *The Ugly Duckling* caught the attention of his boss as well as his colleagues.

This charming rough drawing of young Ferdinand shows Kahl's confidence with a character, whose anatomy is based on the real animal.
© Disney

The sad attitude of the little duckling communicates a level of pathos rarely achieved before in animation. Milt chose this slow, aimless walk to portray loneliness.
© Disney

153

For Disney's first full-length animated feature *Snow White and the Seven Dwarfs*, Milt Kahl teamed up with Eric Larson to choreograph the complex animation of the forest animals that interacted with Snow White. Crowd scenes like these proved technically challenging. For once, the animal groupings needed to read as a cohesive whole, but certain specific animal behaviors had to be acted out.

A dove blushes on the Prince's hand after having delivered a kiss from Snow White.
© *Disney*

An emotionally charged drawing shows a group of animals mourning the death of the princess.
© *Disney*

Following *Pinocchio* it was the film *Bambi* that offered new challenges for supervising animators Frank Thomas, Eric Larson, Ollie Johnston, and Milt Kahl. Walt Disney asked for believable animal characters whose anatomy needed to be based on real deer, rabbits, and birds.

Marc Davis spent many months preparing rough character model sheets showing a successful combination of animal and human characteristics. But it was Milt Kahl who shaped the final appearance for all the deer as well as Thumper, the rabbit. He went on to animate the memorable sequence, where the bunnies challenge young Bambi to leap over a fallen tree.

Bambi moves in very interesting and unusual ways here. His anticipation for the big jump looks like something a dog would do: head down to the ground, rear way up, tail wiggling. He then charges forward, but fails to make it across the tree. After a belly landing, Bambi moves his hind legs across the obstacle, one after the other. They interlock, and for a few moments he wobbles, out of balance on three legs, resulting in another fall. It is this carefully planned awkwardness in the animation that makes the scene so entertaining. Milt knew at any given moment about weight and momentum of all parts of the deer's body. Because of that knowledge, he was able to play up the comedy while maintaining believability.

Milt's knowledge about weight and momentum shines through in the sequence where Bambi is trying to jump over the fallen log.
© Disney

Milt also did most scenes with adult Bambi and Feline, including when those two fall in love. After meeting Feline as a grown-up, Bambi stumbles backward and ends up landing in water. Feline gives him a lick on the cheek and the prince of the forest is smitten. From here on the animation becomes broad and appropriately over-the-top. Bambi's smile is so wide, it looks extreme, but fitting on a cartoon deer with such a realistic design.

A few scenes animated in slow motion follow. Bambi follows Feline, jumping elegantly through clouds—the surreal visual clues are obvious. Here again Milt shows his extraordinary talent for making impossible movements look real. After having studied realistic deer anatomy intensely, he then was able to invent unique motion patterns that looked utterly convincing.

A wide smile for a smitten Bambi.
© *Disney*

Bambi in love.
© *Disney*

C–108

C113

C-X16

156

During the WWII years, Disney Studios were only able to produce short-film material, but even then Milt continued to animate brilliant new characters. The 1943 movie *Saludos Amigos* included a section with Donald Duck and a llama in Peru. In one scene, Donald's flute playing starts to irritate the dancing llama. The result is an example of hilariously timed comedy. The action is broadly animated, but completely believable. The llama moves always show a strong sense of weight. This is a heavy animal with a full coat of fur, and Milt makes great use of this body type. After a spirited Charleston, the llama loses control over his dance moves, a few awkward hops follow before the animal falls to the ground. During these leaps, Milt gives the llama more time when airborne and less time when making contact to the ground. (This is actually the rule of thumb when animating a four-legged animal running or jumping.) On the way up there is always a strong stretch going through the whole body, and when he finally falls down, the big squash on the llama's rear makes for a hard impact and feels very satisfying.

Somehow Milt times these moves so beautifully, and he takes great advantage of overlapping action such as toes, the head, and all that fur. The animation is therefore fluid; it is easy to read on the screen and a joy to watch.

The dancing llama from Saludos Amigos *is a joy to watch.*
© *Disney*

157

For the 1943 propaganda short film *Reason and Emotion*, Milt Kahl contributed beautiful cartoony animation of Emotion, a caveman type, and Reason, a sort of rational bookkeeper.

Jumping from the realism of *Bambi* to broad character animation like this didn't seem to be a problem for Milt at all. Even early on in his career he proved that he could handle a huge range of character concepts and animation styles.

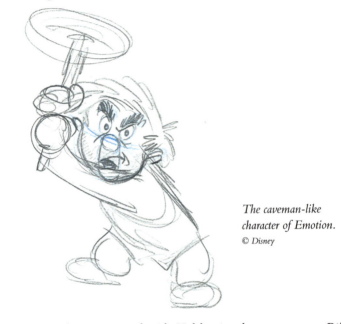

The caveman-like character of Emotion.
© *Disney*

Song of the South was released in 1946, and Milt Kahl turned to story-man Bill Peet's drawings as inspiration for the final designs of the fox, the bear, and the rabbit. Animating these characters turned out to be one of Milt's favorite assignments. The personalities were clearly defined and very contrasting, and Peet's story work provided the animators with outrageous situations.

These anthropomorphic animals gave Milt a chance to be much broader with his animation, something he cherished. The character's voices provided a springboard for razor-sharp timing, yet nothing looks over-animated. Key poses are held long enough to read clearly; it is the transitions to another pose that happen very fast.

*These Kahl sketches show a
perfect and appealing mix of
human and animal traits.*
© *Disney*

159

A model sheet for Pecos Bill made up of Kahl animation drawings.
© *Disney*

Milt animated short film characters like Pecos Bill (1948) along with Ward Kimball, then Johnny Appleseed (1948) with Ollie Johnston. The latter turned out to be a bore to animate, according to Milt. Johnny was just mild-mannered and never showed any strong emotions. Nevertheless his animation is nuanced and appealing.

When Disney returned to full-length animated feature films, starting with *Cinderella* in 1950, Milt was relieved to get back to projects he felt were important. He supervised the animation of the authoritative King as well as the Duke, who is always trying to please. By now Milt had become a very experienced top animator. He was able to not only focus on good character animation, but also on the overall design of each key drawing. Clear silhouette, a balance of straight versus curved lines, and a focus on beautifully drawn hands became a standard of Kahl's work.

The Duke from Cinderella.
© *Disney*

Another character he developed was the warm and sympathetic Fairy Godmother. The fact that she was occasionally absent-minded only enhanced her personality and led to interesting acting.

Milt proved that he was perfectly capable of bringing a character to life whose acting required subtleties and qualities such as compassion and tenderness. The acting is restrained until she begins to use her magic. Then the gestures become broader, and she puts real effort into creating pixie dust with her wand. "Never underestimate the benefit of props," Milt said, and he used the magic wand to enhance the Fairy Godmother's acting. In one scene, while in deep thought, she rests the wand's tip on her cheek. It is a casual gesture that a grandmother might do with her knitting needle.

For *Alice in Wonderland* (1951) Milt designed and animated the title character along with Marc Davis and Ollie Johnston. Carefully based on live-action reference Milt's animation has a simple elegance. "I don't approve of using live action," he stated once, "but if you deal with human characters, it is necessary." He added that if everybody on the movie was a Milt Kahl, it wouldn't be necessary. "But unfortunately they aren't, so it is necessary."

Toward the end of the film, Alice tries to defend herself during the trial. She really comes to life in these Kahl scenes because of her strong emotions. They range from anger and frustration to disbelief. During quick head-turns, the mass of her hair adds overlapping action, and the animation feels loose and real.

"Never underestimate the benefit of props."
© Disney

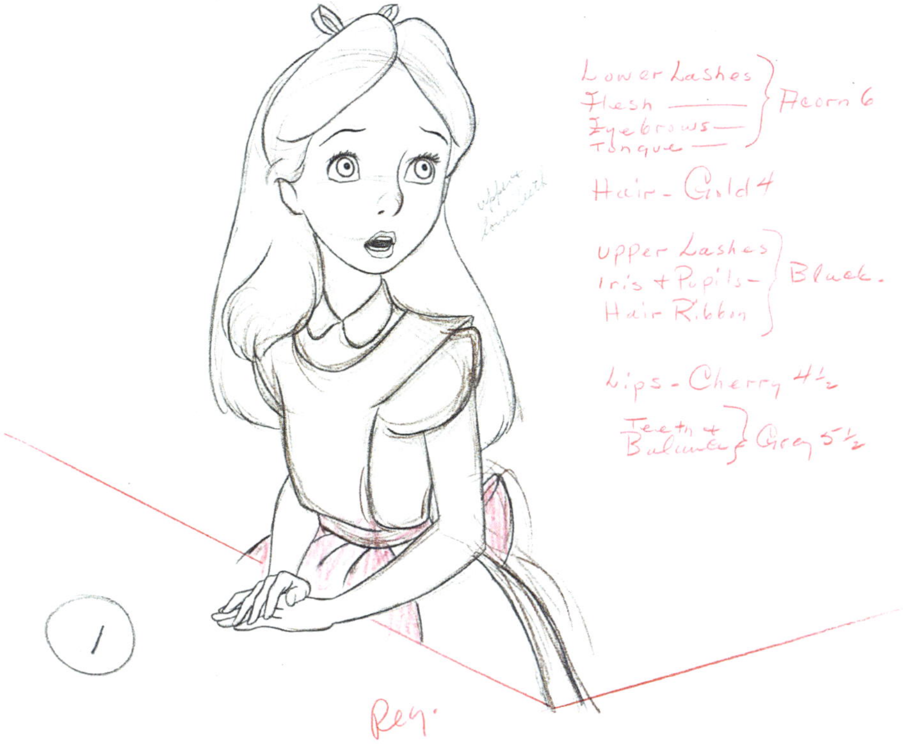

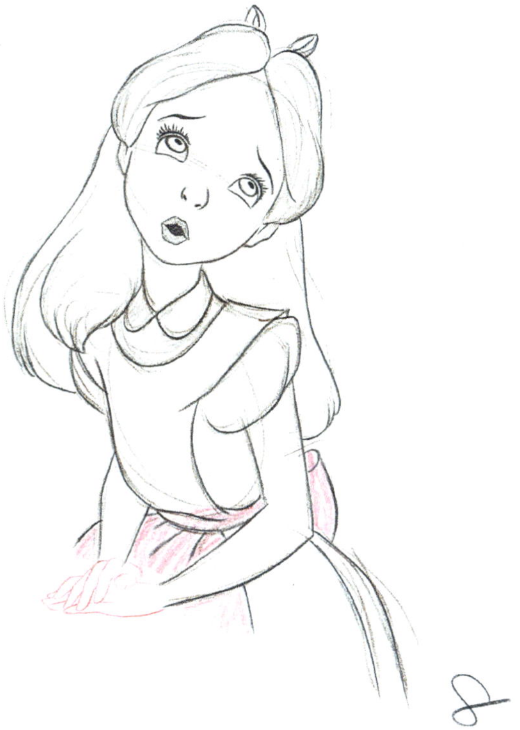

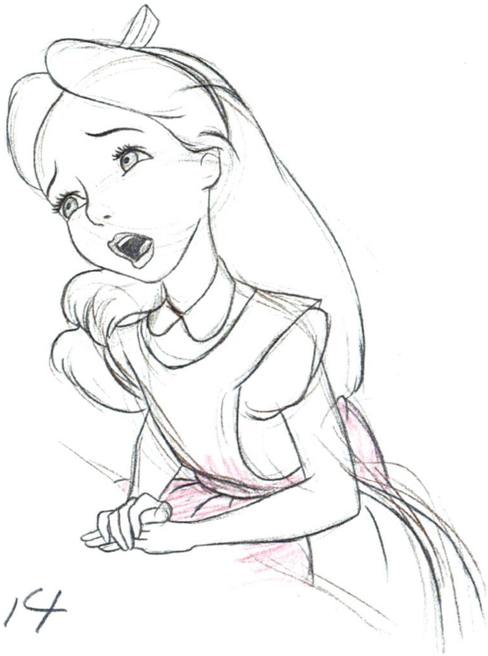

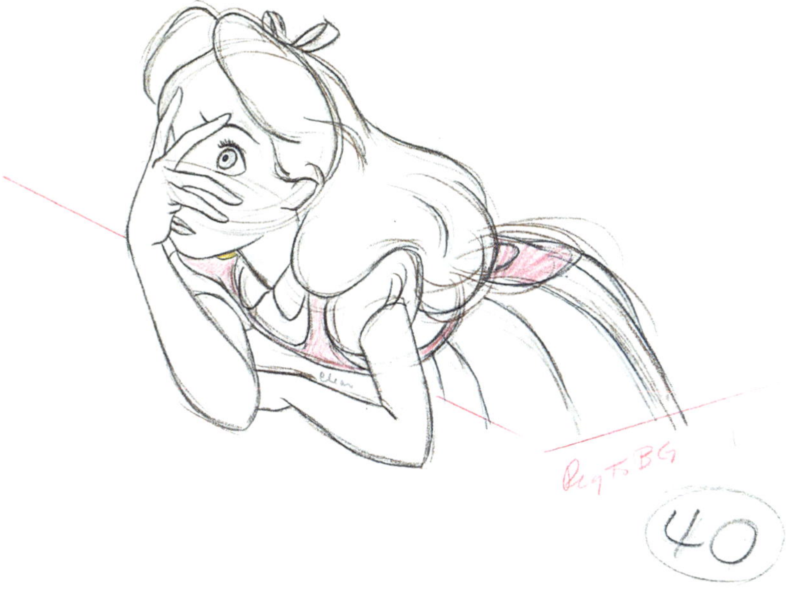

Lower Lashes
Flesh
Eyebrows
Tongue } Acorn 6

Hair - Gold 4

Upper Lashes
Iris + Pupils -
Hair Ribbon } Black.

Lips - Cherry 4½

Teeth +
Baliware } Grey 5½

*Alice displays a range of
emotions during her trial.*
© *Disney*

For the production of *Peter Pan* (1953), Milt had hoped to get assigned to the villain Captain Hook, but Walt Disney had other plans and cast him on Peter Pan and Wendy. It was around that time that Milt started to complain about having to animate the no-fun, straight characters, while his colleagues were assigned to work on much meatier roles. Ward Kimball's response to Milt was: "Yes, but you are so good at that boring stuff!"

Animating Peter Pan was neither challenging nor very interesting according to Kahl, except for the weightless quality when he flies. For a landing, Milt usually had Peter's upper body arrive first while his lower body catches up slowly. The result looks believable, even though the idea of a flying boy is utterly unrealistic. Peter Pan's face is basically a caricature of Bobby Driscoll, who voiced the character. The body proportions show an age somewhere between child and young man, and only Milt drew Peter with just the right amount of realistic anatomy.

Realistic animals were once more required for the animation in *Lady and the Tramp* (1955). Milt designed all of the dog characters, but focused on Tramp along with Frank Thomas.

Early pre-animation character designs for Peter Pan.
© Disney

The introductory scenes of Tramp—waking up in a barrel, then stretching and taking a shower under a rain gutter—are brilliant, arguably some of the best pieces of animation Milt ever did.

Somehow the audience feels what the character is feeling. His exaggerated yawn is infectious and makes you feel tired. The drops of water falling on his head feel cold, because of Tramp's reaction. He jumps forward, then shakes his head, chest, and rear to dry himself. It is the kind of animation that gets the viewer involved, emotionally and physically.

This early introductory scene of Tramp represents some of Milt's best work.
© *Disney*

165

Another realistic assignment was in store for Milt when Walt Disney asked him to supervise Prince Phillip in *Sleeping Beauty* (1959). He did his best to bring this character to life, but pretty much despised doing it. The prince's role in the film didn't call for any interesting emotional changes in his acting. He was just a nice guy who falls in love with the princess; all Milt could do was to draw him in an attractive way and animate him realistically. "Not the type of animation you can get your teeth into," he stated.

The model sheet for the prince shows subtle stylization within carefully designed poses.
© *Disney*

At least he had the opportunity to also animate scenes with King Stefan and King Hubert, who required a broader style of animation. The degree of caricature on these two monarchs is much greater, which allowed for broader acting and more expressive animation.

Heavyset King Hubert usually anticipates any big moves he makes, before his body mass is set in motion. Without this he would float across the screen. Skinny King Stefan is more elegant in his animation; any hand gesture is emphasized by the overlapping action of his large sleeves.

King Hubert and King Stefan provided a chance for expressive animation and contrasting attitudes.
© *Disney*

167

All animators were relieved when a change came about regarding Disney style. The animation drawings in *One Hundred and One Dalmatians* (1961) would not be hand-inked on to cels, but for the first time would be Xeroxed instead. Milt Kahl was thrilled to see his own drawings on the screen, instead of the work of clean-up artists, who he felt often misinterpreted or ruined his original drawings. Milt animated scenes with Pongo and Perdita, but his main focus was the human couple Roger and Anita. Their animation was again based on live-action reference but because of their graphic designs, the motion feels less realistic and more interpreted. The shapes applied in their drawings often look like beautiful paper cut-outs, yet when Anita takes a seat on a couch, some of these shapes overlap in a way a real skirt or an apron would.

Although still based on live-action reference, the graphic design of Anita in One Hundred and One Dalmatians *was a new direction for Milt Kahl.*
© *Disney*

The Sword in the Stone (1963) offered many rich character parts. After setting the style for the film's cast, Milt developed Merlin and Wart as well as Sir Kay and Sir Ector. He then shared sequences starring the comic villain Madame Mim with Frank Thomas. She turned out to be one of Milt's favorites. A cranky, eccentric little witch gave Milt the kind of material he preferred over down-to-earth characters. When Mim introduces herself to Wart, who has been turned into a bird, she breaks into a wild and zany dance that somehow demonstrates her unpredictability.

Milt uses unusual and extreme angles during this scene, which would be difficult to draw for any other animator. Some of his colleagues would say that Milt did this just to challenge himself, others thought that Milt was just showing off his draftsmanship.

Madame Mim turned out to be one of Milt's favorite characters.
© *Disney*

121

99

91

169

The fox from Mary Poppins.
© Disney

Mary Poppins (1964) required a mix of animation and live action. Milt Kahl animated the befuddled little fox, who gets saved from a pack of hunting dogs by Dick Van Dyke.

All of the characters from *The Jungle Book* (1967) were designed by Milt, based on sketches by Bill Peet and Ken Anderson. Except for the elephants, Milt started out doing some animation on all of them.

But the film's powerful villain was all his. Shere Khan is a masterpiece in design, acting, and motion.

Animation had not seen anything like this before. Almost Picasso-esque drawings moving like a real tiger. Knowingly or not, Milt Kahl made a huge personal statement here.

He started out by studying footage from previous Disney live-action movies such as *Jungle Cat* and *A Tiger Walks*. Concept artist Ken Anderson came up with the idea of a suave, above-it-all villain. Milt combined those qualities with a caricature of voice actor George Sanders. The end result is a sly tiger who is holding back his powers only to strike at the very end of the film. Stripes or spots are notoriously difficult and laborious to track on an animated animal, nevertheless they can add tremendous volume and perspective to the animated motion.

A tiger's stripes define the exterior of the animal's body, and in motion they emphasize different areas of its anatomy. Shere Khan moves like a real big cat—when his front feet move through during a walk, the little toe contacts the ground first before the full paw sets down. His back shoulders move up and down drastically, according to which leg is carrying the animal's front weight. His graphic design is extraordinary. You couldn't simplify a big cat's body any more to its essence. Milt knew about the power of his draftsmanship, so when the tiger hits a strong pose, the drawing is held for quite some time. Only the head might move or there could be just an eye blink. Those poses and subtle moves are brilliantly composed to convey power, authority, and arrogance. The less Shere Khan moves, the more intimidating he becomes.

170

Shere Kahn is a masterpiece of subtle personality animation.
© Disney

Milt again concentrated on the human characters for *The Aristocats* (1970). He animated Madame Bonfamille with grace, the lawyer Georges Hautecourt with senior charm, and Edgar the butler with comic villainy.

Milt's human characters for The Aristocats.
© *Disney*

This time around Milt did not refer to live-action for his animation. His opinion by then was that a top animator should know how humans and animals move and shouldn't have to rely on live-action as a crutch. The control he exercises when animating Madame Bonfamille is astounding. Her walk has just the right amount of delicate bounce and feels very natural. The old lawyer shows his age with a knee wobble for each step, but the overall acting is quite energetic since he is still young at heart. The butler's expressions are at times very broad. When he finds out that the cats are to inherit Madame's fortune, his frustration is severe. He mutters "Cats!" and Milt involves the whole face when pronouncing the word. First the mouth opens extremely wide, then closes while eyes and eyebrows form a strong squint.

"Cats!
© *Disney*

173

There are a few memorable moments in the animated sections of *Bedknobs and Broomsticks* (1971). Milt didn't work on the famous soccer game (except for designing the players), but he was responsible for developing the tumultuous relationship between King Leonidas and his assistant, the Secretary Bird.

Ken Anderson provided many sketches before animation for *Robin Hood* (1973) began.

Again Milt Kahl polished and finalized them. He animated key scenes with Robin, Maid Marian, Lady Kluck, and Friar Tuck as well as the rooster Allan-a-Dale and the Sheriff of Nottingham.

Robin Hood as a fox is a very different animal than Brer Fox from *Song of the South*. For once, the Disney style had changed from dimensionally drawn, often cartoony characters to designs that were influenced by modern graphics, and Milt Kahl had more to do with this trend than most artists at the studio. But the acting had changed, too. These animals often demonstrate nuanced, human behavior and the acting is much more subtle than in earlier Disney films.

Brer Fox from 1946.
© *Disney*

Robin Hood from 1973.
© *Disney*

175

Milt Kahl's work method always included precise planning. Before animating, Milt spent a lot of time exploring all possibilities for a scene. He often would stare at a blank sheet of paper for a long time before coming up with small pen or pencil sketches that helped him analyze various ideas for poses and acting patterns. Milt insisted that you need to think about where you are going with the scene before animation begins.

Figuring out ideas for poses and acting patterns.
© Disney

For his final assignment at Disney, Milt took on the villainess Madame Medusa in *The Rescuers* (1977). Being very inspired by Geraldine Page's voice performance, Milt pulled all the stops. He would later say that he probably had more fun animating her than any other character before. Medusa is an animated force to be reckoned with—wildly eccentric while enormously entertaining to watch. No live-action reference was used, her motion is a total creation of the animator. Milt also animated her partner in crime, Mr. Snoops, as well as establishing scenes with the alligators Nero and Brutus. Medusa's design is so unique and individual that only Milt Kahl could draw her. Broad, round shoulders contrast lower arms that look like sticks.

Her soft, flabby body allows for a great range of unusual poses. The expressions Milt invented for her are repulsive and wonderful at the same time.

It is interesting to note that Milt animated most of his acting close-up scenes on "twos," which meant that only 12 drawings per second are seen on the screen, instead of 24. That kind of motion tends to look a little less fluid, but it sure has a crisp snap to it. He also used a mix of ones and twos, depending on what kind of feel a particular motion should have.

Milt Kahl left Disney Studios somewhat prematurely. He was still in top form artistically, but his outspoken, critical point of view on the status of Disney animation was met with resentment and frustration by other artists and management.

Nevertheless he left behind an unparalleled animation legacy of an extremely high standard, which is still admired and studied by fans and professionals today. His drawing style dominated Disney animated films for 40 years and his drive for perfection is inspirational and intimidating at the same time. There is no doubt that the work of Milt Kahl will inspire artists for generations to come.

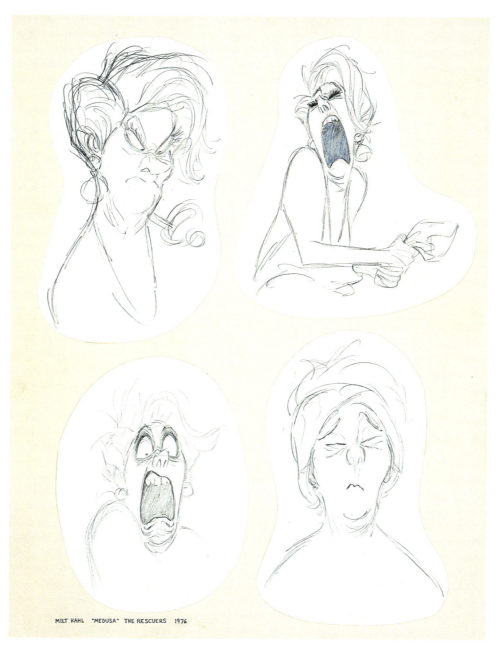

MILT KAHL "MEDUSA" THE RESCUERS 1976

Medusa is an animated force to be reckoned with—wildly eccentric while enormously entertaining to watch.
© *Disney*

179

Pinocchio

1940
PINOCCHIO
ROUGH ANIMATION
Seq. 8.5, Sc.24

The story of Pinocchio takes a dark turn when the title character suddenly realizes that little by little he is turning into a donkey. He had just watched in horror as the boy Lampwick went through the same transformation.

Milt animates Pinocchio turning left and right to show his confusion, ending up in a pose with his back to the camera. At that point the character holds very still, when all of a sudden a tail appears. That isolated piece of action reads very clearly because the tail is the only thing moving at this moment. In realizing his escalating physical change, Pinocchio's body stretches upward. Milt uses this pose in anticipation for the down motion during which Pinocchio grabs the tail and holds it in disbelief.

From a technical point of view, this is a very well-choreographed scene with short pauses, just long enough to show the character's emotion. The audience is left with a feeling of anxiety and suspense.

© Disney

9

13

15

21

25

181

© Disney

*C*inderella

1950
THE GRAND DUKE
ROUGH AND CLEAN-UP ANIMATION
Seq. 5.1, Sc. 193

The Grand Duke is about to leave the home of Lady Tremaine after being informed that no other girl beside Drizella and Anastasia, who did not fit the glass slipper, lives in the house. He turns towards the door while putting on his hat. Suddenly from upstairs a voice appears: "Your grace…" The Duke stops and looks over his shoulder in the direction of the voice.

This is a short scene, but full of personality. It shows Milt Kahl's ability to portray emotions during a brief moment, which otherwise might be considered a second rate continuity scene, a scene of lesser importance.

The Duke's motion and dialogue "Good day… good DAY!" signals that he has had enough of these ladies. The slipper didn't fit, he has wasted his time, and is eager to move to the next house in search of the mystery girl from the ball.

Milt draws a theatrical pose, as the character lifts his hat up high, before putting it firmly on his head. His march-like walk shows determination and annoyance. It offers a nice contrast to the abrupt stop that follows.

© Disney

34

37

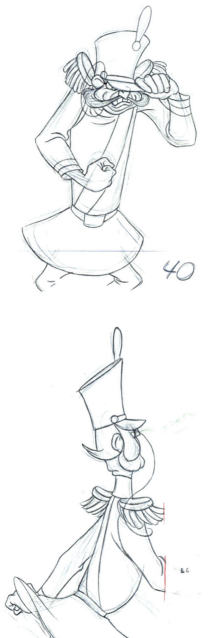

40

51

58

B.G.

62

B.G.

Sleeping Beauty

1959
KING HUBERT AND PRINCE PHILLIP
ROUGH ANIMATION
Seq. 13, Sc. 52

This scene shows Prince Phillip as a character who is capable of projecting strong, even silly emotions. He just told his father, King Hubert, that he met the girl he is going to marry. Phillip then picks up the bewildered king and swirls around in a waltz-like fashion. Technically the scene is a tour de force, which required accurate analysis of the footwork involved in this type of dance.

The way Phillip leans into the action demonstrates his elation as well as playfulness.

Animated without the help of live-action reference, Milt demonstrates his skills for musically choreographed motion. At the time, the scene was met with some criticism by colleagues who questioned the believability of a regularly built person being able to lift up such a heavy character as Hubert.

But the empowering feeling of love enables this animated prince to do the impossible, and to most audiences the scene looked entirely plausible.

It is interesting to see how Hubert's coat was shortened with blue pencil, most likely to enhance the comedy by showing more of his puffy underpants.

© Disney

C149

C155

C174

188

C166

C170

C172

C181

C187

C198

C203

C210

C236

C241

C248

C217

C225

C229

C263

C261

C273

The Aristocats

1970
GEORGES HAUTECOURT
ROUGH ANIMATION
Seq. 4, Sc. 1.1

The introduction of Madame Bonfamille's lawyer Georges Hautecourt is pure delight. He might look like he is 100 years old, but his spirit is youthful and energetic.

After he arrives in his car in front of Madame's house, the lawyer turns off the engine and removes his gloves in rhythm to the tune he is humming. Motion-wise, there is a lot going on at the same time, yet everything reads beautifully as a whole. Hautecourt's head is tilting from side to side as he sings along, while each finger is loosened before a glove is removed. The squash and stretch involved gives the gloves the appearance of soft leather. The same can be said about his face which is full of squishy wrinkles.

The hands' movements are drawn with masterful precision, and the overall bounciness of this performance reveals the character's optimistic personality. He is in a joyful mood and ready to tackle any legal issue coming his way.

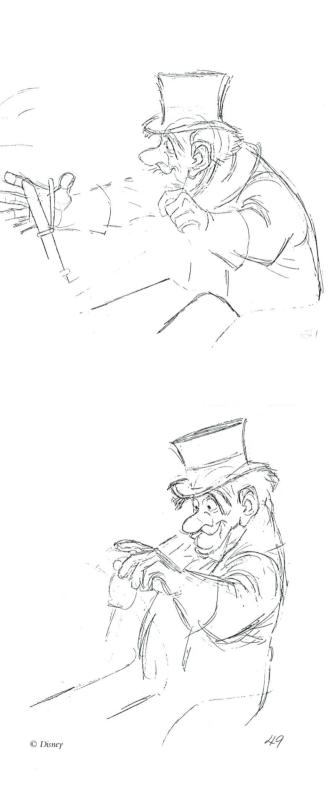

192

© Disney

49

67

110

113

120

The Rescuers

1977
MADAME MEDUSA
ROUGH/CLEAN-UP ANIMATION
Seq. 7, Sc. 300

Medusa just sat down in front of a mirror to remove her make up. She is irritated and furious because the kidnapped girl Penny hasn't been able to find a big diamond for her, called the Devil's Eye. Medusa removes her earrings when she is interrupted by Penny at the door. She immediately changes her attitude from anger to false delight. "Come in, come i-hin!"

Often when there is a strong change in a character's mood, the animator would close the eyes, before opening them with a new expression. This method is a standard for an emotional transition.

For Milt Kahl this approach wasn't good enough. During Medusa's quick mental change he added a couple of deliciously bizarre expressions that still communicate a spiteful annoyance. The audience doesn't fully register these grimaces at the speed of 24 frames per second, but rather feels the character's madness.

As soon as she addresses the girl, Medusa's attitude is completely fake and acted out.

© Disney

111

117

125

129

14

147

161

165

153

157

173

187

Frank Thomas

In the 1995 documentary film *Frank and Ollie*, Frank Thomas voiced his frustration, while looking back over his long career:

> I don't think there was a day going by, where I didn't think I was in the wrong profession, that I should get out of animation. I'd get so mad at something that was going on. Part of the time it was my own inability to draw what I wanted, which all of us had. I guess every artist has that kind of a problem.

A surprisingly candid statement about professional insecurity from one of the world's top character animators. Frank Thomas might not have felt confident about his draftsmanship, but when it came to animated acting performances, he set the bar so high that very few artists ever came close to that level of excellence. Frank's characters are so alive and move in such a natural manner, they seem detached from any animator's conception, they live by themselves and make decisions on their own. Of course it is extremely difficult to achieve screen performances of such a caliber, and Frank Thomas worked harder than most at the studio, according to his colleague Ollie Johnston. While in the Disney training program, a junior animator said of Frank: "You just can't please the guy, he is never satisfied." Within the animation industry, Frank Thomas is known as the Laurence Olivier of animation.

For the first two years at Disney from 1934 to 1936 Frank served as an in-betweener and as an assistant to the great Fred Moore. Fred had made significant breakthroughs in the art of animation, his use of squash and stretch helped Mickey Mouse to appear more believable and charming than ever before. Frank became a serious student of these new animation principles, and by 1936 he was given the chance to do a few scenes with Donald Duck for the short film *Mickey's Circus*.

Captain Donald Duck feeds the circus seals ... or does he?
© Disney

Another example of early Thomas animation is Pluto in *Mickey's Elephant,* also from 1936.

Pluto shows strong emotions, he is annoyed with the antics of a little elephant.
© Disney

Frank Thomas' animation for Little Hiawatha
caught the attention of Walt Disney himself.
© *Disney*

By now Frank Thomas was recognized as a new up-and-comer at the studio, who showed real talent. Walt Disney first took real notice of Frank's outstanding animation when he saw scenes of a little kid encountering a bear cub up close for the 1937 short *Little Hiawatha*. This moment was beautifully staged as they meet in a nose-to-nose confrontation.

Frank still relied on his mentor Fred Moore for help as far as appealing draftsmanship, but the nuanced performance was all his own. Even this early on in Frank's career, his characters move with real weight. The degree of squash and stretch is just right for cartoony characters like these.

And the acting choices reveal that Frank understood and felt their emotions deeply. His philosophy about animating could be summed up as: experience the character's feeling first, then worry about the drawing aspect! In other words, it is the acting the audience will remember, the graphic presentation to a lesser degree.

When it became time to cast animators for Disney's first animated feature *Snow White and the Seven Dwarfs*, Frank Thomas was chosen to be a part of the dwarfs unit.

He animated the section where Snow White orders the dwarfs to wash up before dinner. They all reluctantly leave the house for the outdoor tub, each with their own characteristic walk. Another of Frank's sequences proved to be a breakthrough for animated performances. After Snow White dies, the Seven Dwarfs gather around her body grieving the loss of their beloved princess. There are tears on the screen, and there were tears in the audience. For the first time, animated characters who experience sadness and sorrow deeply affected the viewers like never before.

Delicate facial expressions combined with subtle timing communicate believable emotions of sadness and loss.
© *Disney*

After finishing work on *Snow White*, Frank Thomas retuned to short films featuring Mickey Mouse. *The Brave Little Tailor* from 1938 includes a sequence that is often mistaken as having been animated by Fred Moore. Mickey is being presented to the King and Princess Minnie so he can tell his story about killing seven (giants) in one blow. He enthusiastically acts out the situation in which he found himself surrounded (by houseflies). "They were right on top of me, and then I let them have it," he touts. The audience believes that Mickey is a giant killer, and a huge ovation follows.

Those scenes are arguably the finest as far as character animation goes for Mickey Mouse. There is no doubt that Fred Moore helped out with model drawings here and there, but the acting shows pure Thomas insight and analysis. The motion ranges from very broad to subtle as Mickey exaggerates his efforts in this confrontation. Every gesture and each step the character takes shows believable weight and perspective. The audience is watching living drawings perform.

205

Some of the finest character animation for Mickey Mouse can be found in The Brave Little Tailor.
© *Disney*

206

For the 1939 short film *The Pointer*, Frank animated Mickey facing off with a bear during a hunt. By now the famous Disney character had been given eyes with pupils, which allowed for even greater subtleties and emotional range. The comedic high point is Mickey's attempt to explain his fame to the bear in an effort to be spared.

Walt Disney chose Frank Thomas to be part of the small team of animators that would supervise the animation of the character of *Pinocchio*. Frank's insight into the inner feelings of the living puppet helped to bring him to life during Stromboli's marionette performance. Pinocchio does his best to perform the song "I've Got No Strings," despite his total lack of experience in show business. After an embarrassing fall onstage, the audience starts to laugh at him, but Pinocchio misinterprets their reaction and claps his hands enthusiastically. The whole sequence is full of rich character moments like this one, informing us of Pinocchio's naïve good nature.

Mickey was given eyes with pupils, allowing for greater subtleties and emotional range.
© Disney

207

During production of the film, Frank gave a lecture to fellow animators on how to animate Pinocchio physically. He pointed out that the usual use of squash and stretch is to be avoided, because the character is made out of hard wood. When Pinocchio falls and hits the ground, the body mass must *not* be distorted during contact, instead he just bounces off the floor. This important principle helped to remind viewers that they are looking at a puppet.

Frank Thomas also animated a later sequence in the film, when Pinocchio, now with donkey ears, returns home to find Geppetto gone. He vows to Jiminy Cricket that he will find him, even after finding out that his father had been swallowed by a whale. This is an important turn in Pinocchio's character development—he is starting to show a sense of compassion and responsibility.

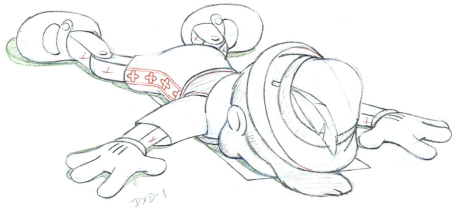

The lack of squash and stretch when Pinocchio falls reminds audiences that he is made out of solid wood.
© Disney

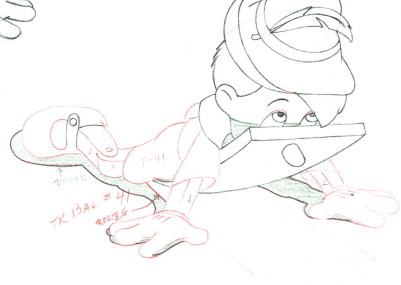

Very few artists were assigned to starting development and early animation for *Bambi.*

Frank Thomas' talents were perfectly suited for a film whose character movements needed to be based on realism, to a degree never attempted before. These deer had to be drawn with real anatomy combined with tasteful caricature. Walt asked the animators to produce test footage; it seems like he was not entirely sure if he would get the results he was hoping for. Frank did rough animation of the scene involving Thumper as he is trying to teach Bambi how to say the word "bird." In the process, Bambi mistakes a butterfly, who happens to fly by, for a bird, and he begins to chase it enthusiastically. After a few erratic moves, typical for a young faun, the butterfly lands gently on Bambi's tail. The scene communicates poetry in motion. The superb animation has elegance and an almost dance-like choreography—Disney animation at a new artistic highpoint.

Perfectly staged and animated, this charming scene became an iconic image for the film.
© *Disney*

209

The very important sequence featuring Bambi and Thumper on ice was almost cut from the film as it was considered extraneous. Frank argued and fought to keep this section in the movie, knowing full well that this story material offered rich possibilities for personality animation. The contrast alone between the two characters couldn't be greater. Thumper moves like a professional skater, while Bambi keeps falling over and over again, and Thumper's instructions aren't helpful at all. Frank animated the comedic antics of these two in a completely believable way. Whether the movement is subtle or broad, there is always weight, and therefore the characters look like real creatures. Today it is difficult to imagine the film without this highly entertaining sequence.

A rough layout pose shows Thumper's confidence on the ice.
© *Disney*

During the 1941 labor strike at The Walt Disney Studios Walt accepted an invitation by the US government to go on a goodwill tour of South America. Accompanied by a small group of artists, that trip also presented useful inspiration for the upcoming production of a series of short films based on Latin folklore and culture. Frank Thomas was a member of this traveling crew as the only animator. He helped design characters like the parrot José Carioca and the little Gauchito with his flying Burrito. Back in Burbank, Frank animated brilliant key sequences for the 1945 short film *The Flying Gauchito*. The main challenge was how to combine characteristics of a donkey with those of a bird for this fantasy creature.

Sketches for
The Flying Gauchito.
© *Disney*

During WWII, Frank worked on a few propaganda short films like *The Winged Scourge* (1943), starring the Seven Dwarfs, and *Education for Death* (1943), which required character animation of Adolf Hitler.

After the war Walt Disney released *The Adventures of Ichabod and Mr. Toad* in 1949. The film presents two very different stories: one originates from English literature, the other is an American folktale. For the Mr. Toad section, which was based on the book *The Wind in the Willows* by Kenneth Grahame, Frank Thomas' strong sense for character relationships came through in the sequence that introduced Toad to the audience. Rat and Mole are confronting Toad in an effort to talk some sense into their friend, who has been ignoring his responsibilities for Toad Hall. Instead he has chosen a lifestyle of carefree fun as he rides along out on the open road on his horse Cyril. The contrast between these personality duos is ideal for entertaining animation. Rat is sensible and serious, Mole is trying to be, while Toad and Cyril are utterly irresponsible without a care in the world. Rat's body language is composed and businesslike, Toad's acting shows broad, theatrical gestures that communicate a zest for life.

Frank explores range and flexibility within Toad's body.
© *Disney*

211

The Ichabod Crane section offered Frank a sequence with an opportunity for all-out tour de force acting. Toward the end of the film, after attending Katrina's party, Ichabod rides home through a dark forest. It is nighttime, and the Headless Horseman is very much on his mind thanks to Brom Bones' impersonation of this legendary figure at the party. The sights and sounds of the forest bring out fear and eventually horror in Ichabod's mind, but there is always the element of comedy in the way he reacts to the intimidating surroundings. He swallows nervously, covers his head with his lanky arms, and hangs on to his horse tightly.

This is not easy footage to animate—whatever Ichabod's action might be has to be coordinated with the horse's swaggering walk. Frank did this brilliantly, and it is astounding to find out that he animated this sequence at the super-fast rate of 40 to 50 feet per week. Incredible!

Frank animated this Ichabod Crane sequence
at the rate of 40 to 50 feet per week.
© Disney

Walt Disney surprised Frank Thomas when he assigned him the villainous stepmother Lady Tremaine for the film *Cinderella*. "I had been known for cute, appealing characters. This was a very different kind of personality." Frank knew about the challenge it would take to bring the stepmother to life. In order to be convincing, she had to be handled subtly and realistically. He got some help from actress Eleanor Audley, whose chilling voice performance inspired Frank a great deal. She also provided live-action reference, and Frank incorporated some of her nuanced acting into his animation. Frank later commented on the dangers that live-action footage could present. If photostats (printed frames of the filmed live performance) are being traced blindly, the animation will look soft and mushy. Actors have a tendency to slowly shift their weight from one leg to the other, something that rarely works in graphic motion. The animator needs to edit the live footage and find an essence within the acting. Usually poses need to be strengthened and the timing requires more contrast. Often whole sections are not being used at all because the animator found better ways for bringing the performance across.

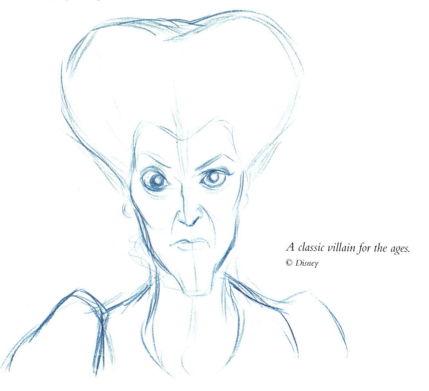

A classic villain for the ages.
© *Disney*

213

Lady Tremaine's subtle movements help to establish her truly evil personality.
© *Disney*

Cinderella's stepmother is a perfect example of a villain who becomes much more evil and powerful by moving very little. Holding a certain pose or a specific expression allows the animator to show the character thinking. One of Lady Tremaine's most powerful moments occurs early on in the film, when she confronts Cinderella while having breakfast in bed. She smilingly delivers an endless list of household chores; only occasionally does she change her expression to make fierce eye contact, reinforcing her impossible demands. A classic villain for the ages.

Frank Thomas animated a less realistic and much more comedic villainess for the next feature film *Alice in Wonderland* from 1951. The Queen of Hearts presented an interesting problem to the animator. How do you balance menace and comedy within her personality? Both were needed, and Frank struggled originally with these opposing qualities.

He eventually found a live version of this character while playing the piano with the Disney-Dixieland-Band Firehouse Five Plus Two. The group was performing on the island of Catalina when Frank spotted a heavyset lady in the audience. At times she was brash when talking to her husband, but she also had a dainty side to her when drinking a cup of tea. Frank all of a sudden had a person to base his new character on. Severe mood swings from one second to the next became a trademark for Frank's brilliant animation. When the Queen gets angry, she loses all control and gestures wildly. During her composed moments, she usually shows a fake, smirky smile.

Frank originally struggled finding the balance between the menace and the comedy for the Queen of Hearts.
© *Disney*

215

Because the Queen of Hearts didn't have much screen time, Frank was able to animate another character, the talking Doorknob. He interacts with Alice early on in the movie, when his door blocks the girl from following the White Rabbit. His animation is astounding, considering that this character is only a prop, an inanimate object. Frank gives him a full range of expressions, and on top of that he is able to maintain a keyhole for any mouth shape during his dialogue.

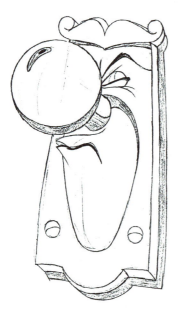

A full range of expressions for Alice in Wonderland's *talking Doorknob.*
© Disney

There was more than one animator who wanted to draw Captain Hook, the villain in the 1953 film *Peter Pan*. Milt Kahl desperately lobbied for the assignment. But Walt Disney had Frank Thomas in mind, an animator with outstanding acting skills. Again there were two different character qualities that needed to work in unison. Some story artists had developed sequences showing Hook as a snobbish connoisseur of fine things, others showed him as a rough pirate.

Frank combined both approaches to create an entertaining villain, who could also be a real threat.

Through interaction with his sidekick Smee, who is also his confidant, we find out about Hook's motives. He is driven by his goal to get rid of Peter Pan. Hans Conried voiced the character and acted out scenes for the animators. Frank used some of this reference carefully, starting with Hook's introduction. He is studying a map trying to figure out Pan's hiding place. The gestures are broad when he is frustrated; they become more subtle as certain ideas come to his mind.

The animation never feels like it is based on live-action reference, the final acting choices were made by the animator.

Hook is looking for Peter Pan's hiding place.
© *Disney*

217

There are many brilliant sequences that give us insight into Hook's personality. At one point he sweet-talks Tinker Bell into revealing Pan's whereabouts. For a moment Hook becomes impatient and aggressive, but then catches himself to change his attitude again. "Continue, my dear!"

Frank was excellent at portraying complex mood swings, he often used irregular eye blinks to ease into the next attitude.

Frank excelled at showing Hook's mood swings.
© *Disney*

For the film *Lady and the Tramp*, Frank Thomas animated important acting scenes with the leading dog characters. He developed Tramp along with Milt Kahl. Being a dog-owner for much of his life, Frank had already observed dog anatomy and behavior at home before he started on this assignment. In one of his memorable sequences, Tramp introduces himself to Lady, Jock, and Trusty, who are discussing the upcoming arrival of a human baby. Tramp interrupts the conversation and explains what a nuisance this newcomer to the family will be.

Frank plays off the contrast between the characters beautifully. Lady doesn't quite know what to make of this street-smart intruder, while Jock and Trusty do their best to get this pesky dog off the property. Those scenes give us great insight into their personalities.

In this layout sketch Frank positions the dogs effectively as a group.
© *Disney*

It is not an overstatement to say that when Lady and Tramp share a spaghetti dinner in a romantic setting, movie history was made. Frank Thomas was the perfect animator to handle a sequence like this one. He turned what could have been an unappealing, messy situation into one of the greatest love scenes of all time. Beautiful draftsmanship, subtle animation, and insightful acting brought this moment to life in a way that no other animator could have done.

The look the two characters exchange toward the end of the dinner makes everybody believe that they have fallen in love. The scene became iconic not only for romance in film, but also for the power of Disney animation.

One of the most charming moments ever animated.
© *Disney*

221

The three fairies have very different personalities.
© Disney

Frank teamed up with colleague Ollie Johnston to animate the three good fairies Flora, Fauna, and Merryweather for the film *Sleeping Beauty*. Both animators didn't agree with Walt Disney's original concept for these characters. He thought of them as sharing the same kind of personality, somewhat like Donald Duck's nephews Huey, Dewey, and Louie. Ollie and Frank argued that contrasting characteristics would make for a much more interesting trio. So Flora became the bossy leader, Fauna takes a little time to grasp a situation, and Merryweather is the most pugnacious one.

Perhaps because of their less realistic character design, the fairies are animated in a looser style than the rest of the cast. Their body shapes and facial features allowed for more expressive acting. Some live-action reference was used, but it is not evident in the final animated performances.

Frank helped supervise the animation of Pongo and Perdita in Disney's *One Hundred and One Dalmatians*. Even though many animators were by now experienced in the motion of dogs, adult Dalmatians along with a few puppies were brought to the studio for study. Frank analyzed their specific proportions as well as bone and muscle structure.

Sketches showing the proportions and physical makeup of Dalmatians.
© *Disney*

He animated charming scenes such as Pongo and Perdita's decision to leave home to go on a search for their puppies. Later on they reunite with them in a barn in the company of cows.

One lovely scene stands out when one of the puppies, having positioned himself on top of his father, slides down his back. The way Pongo's soft skin reacts to the puppy's weight shows the believable contact between the two bodies.

Frank also animated the dogs experiencing some difficulties when they continue their journey on a frozen creek. Trying to walk on an icy surface is something Frank was famil-iar with since his animation of Bambi a couple of decades earlier.

The Sword in the Stone gave Frank Thomas the opportunity to work on a variety of characters.

A charming moment from One Hundred and One Dalmatians. *© Disney*

He animated both Merlin and Madam Mim, as they prepare for the wizards' duel. Mim sets the rules for the fight (she actually makes them up on the spur of the moment). Those scenes rank among Frank's best acting scenes ever. Mim is utterly convincing as she gestures theatrically. Merlin remains skeptical and adds a rule or two himself. As the two begin to change themselves into different animals in an attempt to outdo each other, we see Frank Thomas as an animator of action scenes. The chase is timed very sharply, and the individual transformations are inventive and entertaining.

Another highlight in the film was also animated by Frank. At one point Merlin magically turns himself and young Wart into squirrels. He wants the boy to find out what life is like for a small creature of the forest. Things become complicated when a young

girl squirrel shows her affection for Wart. Merlin finds a
female admirer as well, and both of them do their best
to escape these love-struck females. The whole sequence
is about love, which can be passionate, silly, or disap-
pointing. Frank later commented that the squirrel section was one of his favorite assignments at Disney.

Frank was excellent at animating dances, and he
had the chance to show this skill in the 1964 film *Mary
Poppins*, where four penguins were paired with actor Dick
Van Dyke. Since the live-action footage was filmed first, Frank
needed to be very careful in his animation to avoid collisions between a penguin and Dick
Van Dyke. When the actor's leg would swing sideways, the nearest penguin had to duck or
jump over the leg to get out of the way. One might think that this could result in awkward
choreography, but Frank actually took advantage of this challenge, and these little missteps
added a wonderful and natural quality to the overall dance.

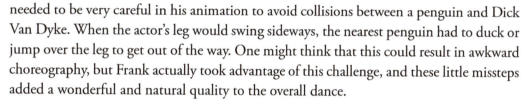

This sequence from The
Sword in the Stone *was
one of Frank's favorite
Disney assignments.*
© *Disney*

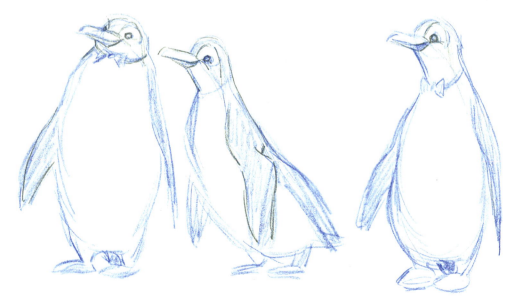

*Three of the penguins
who do their best
to keep up with
Dick Van Dyke.*
© *Disney*

225

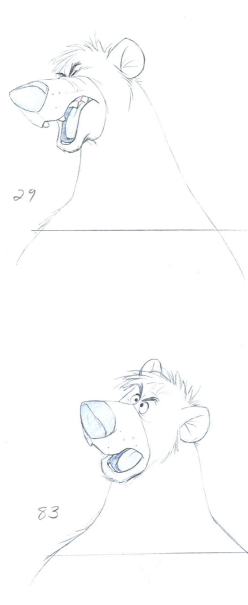

Frank Thomas and Ollie Johnston were again paired to develop the intricate relationship between the man-cub Mowgli and Baloo the bear in *The Jungle Book*.

After these two characters meet, Baloo tries to teach Mowgli to behave like a bear. He challenges him to a boxing match. The boy gradually takes a liking to this carefree bear, and a beautiful friendship begins. Frank animated those poignant scenes, which rival any relationship from a live action film. Eventually Bagheera, the panther, catches up with them to question Baloo's decision to take care of Mowgli. "And just how do you think he will survive?" he asks the bear. Baloo's response is hilarious. He mocks Bagheera by repeating his question: "How do you think he will… what do you mean, how do you think?" He is obviously ticked off, and Frank found just the right attitude in his animation to communicate it.

Baloo, being upset at Bagheera,
responds by mimicking him.
© *Disney*

The characters' contrasting attitudes communicate clearly in this one sketch.
© Disney

Later in the film, Frank animated a deeply emotional scene, when Baloo is trying to tell Mowgli that he is taking him to the man village. The bear still doubts whether this was the right decision and he is trying to find the right words, anticipating Mowgli's reaction to what he is about to announce. Only a master actor like Frank is capable of portraying a character with these complex, conflicting emotions.

227

Frank Thomas' animation added a comedic touch to the sinister song "Trust In Me." Kaa, the python, tries to hypnotize Mowgli with the intention of having him for dinner. Luckily the tiger Shere Khan interrupts just in time. Frank also animated important personality scenes with King Louie, the orangutan.

The next film, *The Aristocats*, offered Frank a variety of character assignments. He animated the romantic get together with alley cat Thomas O'Malley and the aristocratic Duchess. The sequence never reaches the originality and entertainment of *Lady and the Tramp*, but the animation is believable and fun to watch. Other characters who benefitted from the Thomas touch were the butler Edgar and the geese. Frank's most memorable animation in the film is probably in the sequence that features the country dogs Napoleon and Lafayette as they try to settle for the night in their stolen motorcycle sidecar. They are constantly interrupted by Edgar, who attempts to retrieve incriminating evidence he had left at the crime scene. The two dogs act like an old couple, constantly bickering and finding fault with the other one.

The two canine stars from
The Aristocats.
© *Disney*

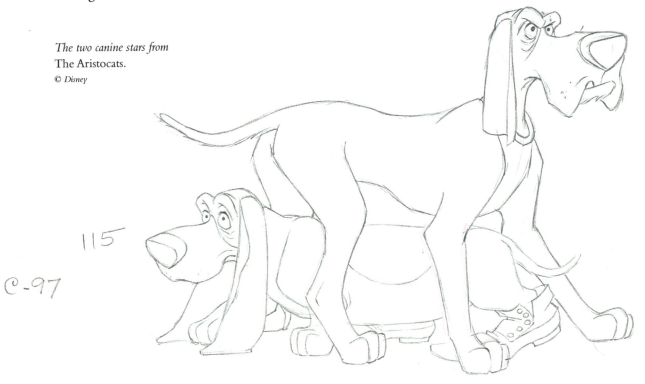

FIELD

FIELD

e-157

Frank Thomas admitted that working on the movie *Robin Hood* was not a favorite assignment. There wasn't a character he could fully develop, instead he helped out on various sequences that needed solid performances. When Robin Hood disguises himself as a stork to participate in the archery contest, Frank animated a character acting as someone else. Normally this would be an animator's dream, but the story artists didn't provide for the kind of situations that would translate into rich character animation. That being said, Frank's performance of Robin as a stork is convincing to an audience. The fact that Prince John as well as the Sheriff of Nottingham at first buy into the masquerade seems believable.

A convincing disguise
for Robin Hood.
© Disney

229

*Reluctant agents
Bernard and Bianca.
© Disney*

The Rescuers is a film with a cast mostly made of small critters, and Frank had his hand in animating many of them, such as the lead couple Bernard and Bianca. Mice had often taken on comedic roles in Disney animation, but these two needed to have leading star qualities.

Their acting became less mouse-like and more human-like in order to carry the romantic as well as the adventure elements of the story in a believable way. Frank animated the charming sequence when Bianca chooses janitor Bernard to be her co-agent for the mission to find Penny, the orphan girl. He also drew the alligators Nero and Brutus, as they chase the mice while frantically playing the organ. Many scenes with the swamp animals, including Ellie Mae and Luke were also animated by Frank.

The Fox and the Hound (1981) was Frank Thomas' final film. He worked on it for about one year, animating the pups Tod and Copper as they meet and play.

It is arguably the one sequence in the film that feels like vintage Disney. The motion is believable, and the acting is based on real children, having fun.

After retiring from animation, Frank and his friend Ollie Johnston started to write a series of important books on the techniques and philosophy of Disney animation. We are very lucky that these two men left their knowledge and wisdom in print. Animation is a complex art form that involves the study of many things, something that can be confusing and intimidating to any student of the medium. These books don't offer any shortcuts or tricks, but they spell out what is involved in becoming a top animator: observing the world around you and interpreting human and animal nature through your characters.

The young Tod and Copper from The Fox and the Hound, *Frank Thomas' final film.*
© Disney

Frank Thomas' own animation is unique on many levels. From a technical point of view, it is interesting to note that when studying any one of Frank's scenes, it is almost impossible to find definitive key drawings—the ones that frame the action and tell the story. To Frank, every drawing was important, they were all keys to him. He hardly ever moves into what is nowadays called a "golden pose." Even within an important position, there is subtle movement to keep the animation alive. The motion never stops; perhaps that's why Frank Thomas' characters are living, breathing creations.

The Adventures of Ichabod and Mr. Toad

1949
BROM BONES AND TILDA
CLEAN-UP OVER ROUGH ANIMATION
Seq. 7, Sc. 36

Frank Thomas had been known for his fine, subtle character acting, but here he shows that he is perfectly comfortable with broad action and comedy.

During the Thanksgiving Party, Brom Bones is in pursuit of Katrina Van Tassel, who is dancing with Ichabod Crane. Brom invites little Tilda to a dance, in hopes he can swap her with Katrina. Once a dancing item, however, Tilda vehemently resists any attempts to get separated from her handsome partner. Brom's frustrated efforts to free himself lead to acrobatic as well as hilarious actions. As he tries to pull his hand from Tilda's grip, his finger elongates for one frame. It's a wonderful and surreal moment that signals that Brom Bones can't win; Tilda is impossible to shake off. As the scene continues and the motion escalates, the girl manages to stay attached to Bones, having a great time along the way.

The overlapping movement of the characters' hair and clothing helps to make this frantic dance look fluid and believable.

© Disney

233

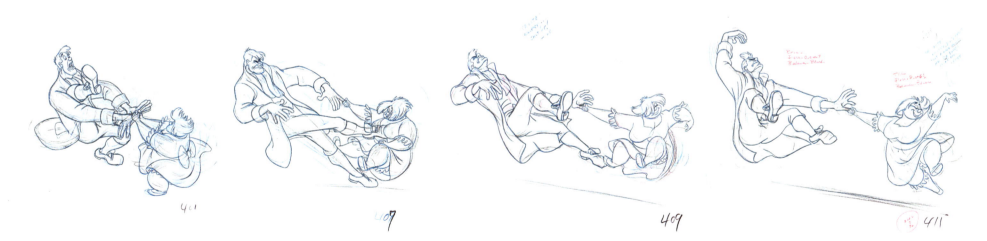

Alice in Wonderland

1951
QUEEN OF HEARTS
ROUGH ANIMATION
Seq. 11, Sc. 29

These few rough key drawings demonstrate the Queen's volatile temperament and her abrupt mood swings. During the trial sequence, she startles Alice with her erratic reactions. At the start of the scene the Queen seems pleased: "Yes, my child…" Then suddenly her attitude changes and she bellows: "Off with her… [head]".

She is interrupted by the little King who is pulling on her dress to get her attention in order to propose a different path for the trial.

Frank draws explosive, seemingly uncontrolled gestures before the Queen freezes in mid action. It takes her a moment to realize that she has been interrupted by somebody. The contrast in the scene's timing with its fast and slow bits surprises not only Alice, but the audience as well. A most unpredictable character!

© Disney

236

38

52

58

66

74

Peter Pan

1953
CAPTAIN HOOK
CLEAN-UP ANIMATION
Seq. 11, Sc. 4

After capturing Tinker Bell, Captain Hook tries to gain the little pixie's trust.

He admits defeat against Peter Pan. "Tomorrow I leave the island!" he promises in a grand theatrical, almost campy gesture. The scene is effectively staged from Tinker Bell's point of view and requires Hook to be drawn in an up-shot. Particularly his last pose, which shows him rising up in perspective, puts the viewer at a low eye-level.

This is Hook, the actor, who has no intention of departing the next day.

Drawing from this angle could present a challenge for the animator. Foreshortening Hook's elongated head is not an easy thing to do, but Frank knew that it was necessary to present the character in a high, superior position.

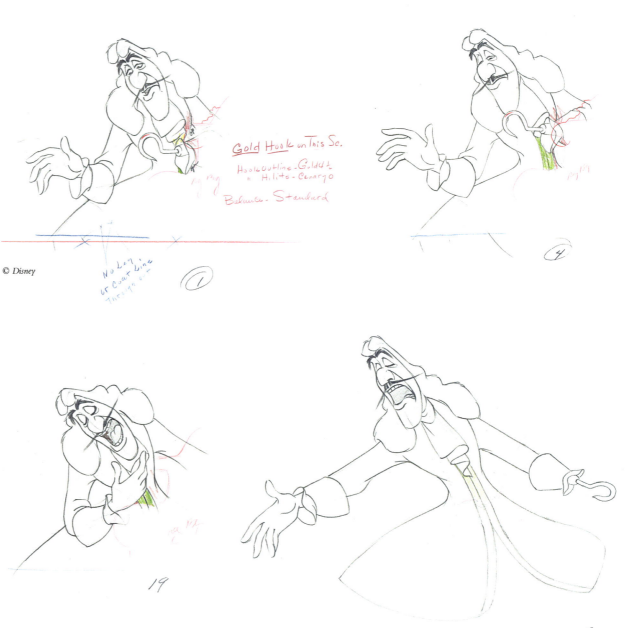

© Disney

11

14

17

31

33

239

Sleeping Beauty

1959
MERRYWEATHER
ROUGH ANIMATION
Seq. 7, Sc. 12

After Maleficent's curse on the Princess Aurora, the three good fairies try to decide what to do next. Tea and cookies magically appear as the discussion about the evil witch continues. Merryweather suddenly bursts: "I'd like to turn her into a fat ol' hop toad!"

Frank takes full advantage of the scene's acting opportunities. During the first part of the dialogue, Merryweather works herself into a squashed position with shoulders raised and head lowered. This pose serves as a strong anticipation for the jump that follows. For a second it seems Merryweather turns herself into a hop toad. The chubby fairy's body stretches as it shoots upward. When completely airborne all her body parts become compressed before landing back on the chair. The fact that a drop of tea leaves her cup on the way down adds a nice touch.

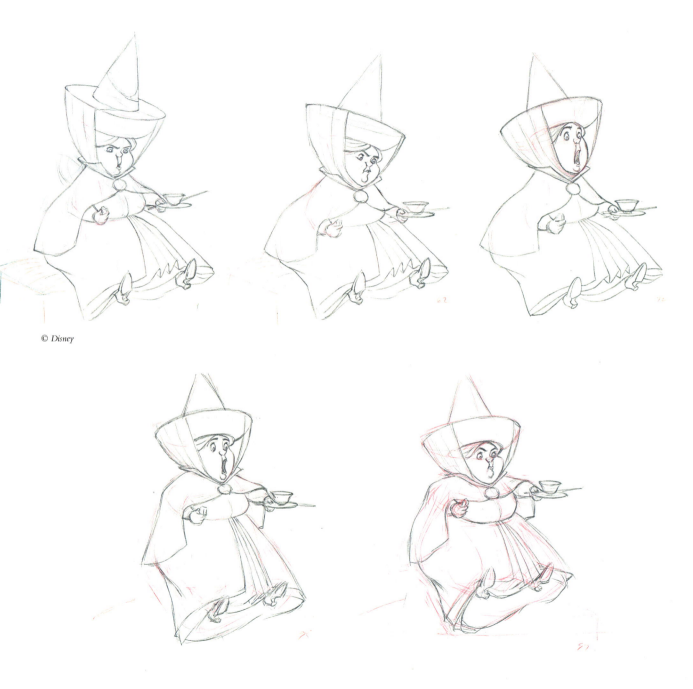

© Disney

240

The Sword in the Stone

1963
MADAM MIM
ROUGH ANIMATION
Seq. 10, Sc. 13.1

In this scene, Madam Mim continues to make up the rules about what and what not to turn into for the upcoming wizards duel with Merlin: "[Rule one, no mineral or vegetable]… only animal. Rule two, no make believe things like pink dragons and stuff. Now…"

Mim feels in charge here and is confident she will be the winner of this battle, knowing very well that she is going to cheat. Her theatrical poses display a sense of the fun she is having. When pink dragons come to mind, her hands gesture wildly to emphasize that those would be forbidden creatures to turn into.

Drawing-wise Frank, might have struggled a bit trying to get the head angles and hand positions just right, but as always he succeeds in orchestrating an interesting acting pattern that communicates the character's true feelings. Mim's emotion here is a sort of playful overconfidence.

242

© *Disney*

21

29

39

87

95

120

© Disney

122   127   131

143   145

Ollie Johnston

*O*llie *J*ohnston always felt that the characters he animated were living beings. "I never thought of them as just lines on paper—to me Pinocchio, Bambi, and Mickey really existed," he stated once.

It is that conviction that led to a very personal approach toward animation, one where the animator analyzes and eventually identifies with the character's emotions. Those feelings become the springboard for what the drawings will look like and how they will move on the screen.

Ollie never considered a particular design style that a film might call for to be a dominant factor in his animation. It was always the core of the character's emotional state he was trying to get to more than anything. That insight was the most important thing that motivated him. "If the animator doesn't understand what the character is feeling, the audience won't either," he said.

Most young animators tend to overlook this important aspect when trying to create believable animation.

The temptation to get started right away and draw before analyzing what is going on in the character's mind is often too great. But those scenes will only show graphic motion, nicely executed perhaps, but void of any real emotional impact on viewers.

Applying Ollie's philosophy can be a game-changer for many animators who are unsure of why their animation isn't "coming off the screen" like classic Disney films do. It might sound simplistic, but when Ollie says: "Don't animate drawings, animate feelings!" there is a profound meaning to those words. The idea is to learn how to draw so well that you don't have to think about the quality of your draftsmanship as much, instead you need to focus on the characters' performance. Animate from the inside out, understand and feel what they go through.

It is often helpful to search among one's own family or circle of friends for inspiration. Do I have an uncle or a cousin who has a similar personality to the character I am animating? What would my uncle do in a situation like this one? Observing people's behavior in real life is a tremendous asset to an animator's work.

After Ollie Johnston arrived at Disney in 1935 he was put to work as an in-betweener, which was common for any newcomer. It was a way for the studio to find out about the young artist's discipline, level of drawing, and work ethics. After in-betweening on several shorts, Ollie caught the eye of animator Fred Moore, who was looking for a new assistant. Production on *Snow White and the Seven Dwarfs* was about to begin, and Ollie ended up not only in-betweening Moore's scenes, but also doing clean-up work on the dwarfs before eventually animating a few scenes himself. Ollie was in awe of his mentor's talent; "Fred just couldn't make a drawing that wasn't appealing." He also learned that part of what made a Moore scene look so alive was the fact that strong visual changes were taking place within his characters. The amount of body mass always remained the same but by treating it like a flexible water balloon, new life was added to otherwise stiff-looking animation.

Ollie took full advantage of this principle when he was given a few scenes featuring various townspeople to animate for the 1939 Mickey short *The Brave Little Tailor*.

Early work on The Brave Little Tailor. © *Disney*

249

Walt Disney saw plenty of promise in Ollie's work, and soon the young animator joined colleagues Frank Thomas and Milt Kahl to help supervise the animation of the character of Pinocchio. While some of the film's story and design issues were being addressed, Ollie did animation for short films like *The Pointer*, *The Practical Pig*, and *Mickey's Surprise Party*.

Fred Moore's influence is evident in these early Johnston scenes.

Mickey is on the lookout for a bear.
© Disney

Three naughty wolves cause all kinds of trouble for the little pigs.
© Disney

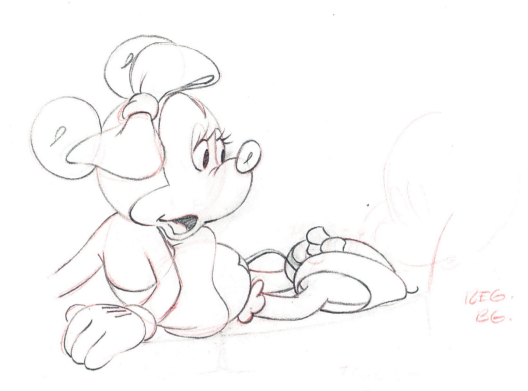

Ollie's versions of two Disney superstars.
© *Disney*

Pinocchio might be made out of wood, but he acts like a real kid.
© *Disney*

Ollie's concept for Pinocchio's personality was that of a well-meaning, naïve little boy:

"All he wanted to do is please his father Geppetto, but his lack of life experiences got him into trouble. After all, he had just been born." The sequence in the film when Pinocchio comes to life was animated by Ollie, but Fred Moore still lent a hand when appeal and drawing needed to be strengthened.

Another section of the film that benefited from the Johnston touch was Pinocchio's conversation with the Blue Fairy in Stromboli's wagon. As Pinocchio tries to make excuses for not going to school, his nose starts to grow, the punishment for lying. The acting is subtle here; Pinocchio goes back and forth from being bewildered by his nose change to still trying to convince the Blue Fairy of his innocence. It is clear to the audience that he is very uncomfortable throughout the scene, because deep inside he knows that not telling the truth is probably a bad thing.

Pinocchio's nose begins to grow.
© *Disney*

A makeup moment in the "Pastoral" sequence.
Clean-up artists would later add floral covers to
the topless centaurettes.
© *Disney*

While Ollie's teammates Frank Thomas and Milt Kahl moved over to the *Bambi* unit, he was asked to help supervise the animation of cupids and centaurettes for the *Pastoral* sequence in *Fantasia*. These sexy fantasy creatures had been designed by Fred Moore, and Ollie brought them to life with feminine grace. He later recalled enjoying their "makeup" moments, when cupids apply lipstick and rouge to the girls' faces. Originally animated topless, the clean-up artists later added floral covers in order to appease family audiences.

253

When story work for *Bambi* was finalized, Ollie and the other animators went to work and produced some of the most heartwarming and enchanting animated pieces of personality animation ever done. Particularly the motion of the deer characters has an almost poetic quality to it. Because these movements are often synchronized to music, the result looks elegant and balletic. One of those scenes was animated by Ollie. At the beginning of the movie, some time is spent showing how the young faun is still unsteady on his legs, and has difficulties balancing his steps. Bambi has just fallen to the ground yet again, and all the bunnies excitedly encourage him to stand up. With all this encouragement he is determined to show them that he is very much capable of walking. Bambi's back is staged toward camera, we see him placing his weight on his left rear leg, then the right and left again, as his upper body rises up. There is definitely some effort that goes into getting up this way. He then proceeds to walk away from camera, followed by several bunnies. If there is such a thing as "poetry in motion" then this scene is it. Bambi gets into these beautiful poses on specific musical beats. Motion and music perfectly complement each other.

Bambi's early attempt to walk was poetry in motion.
© *Disney*

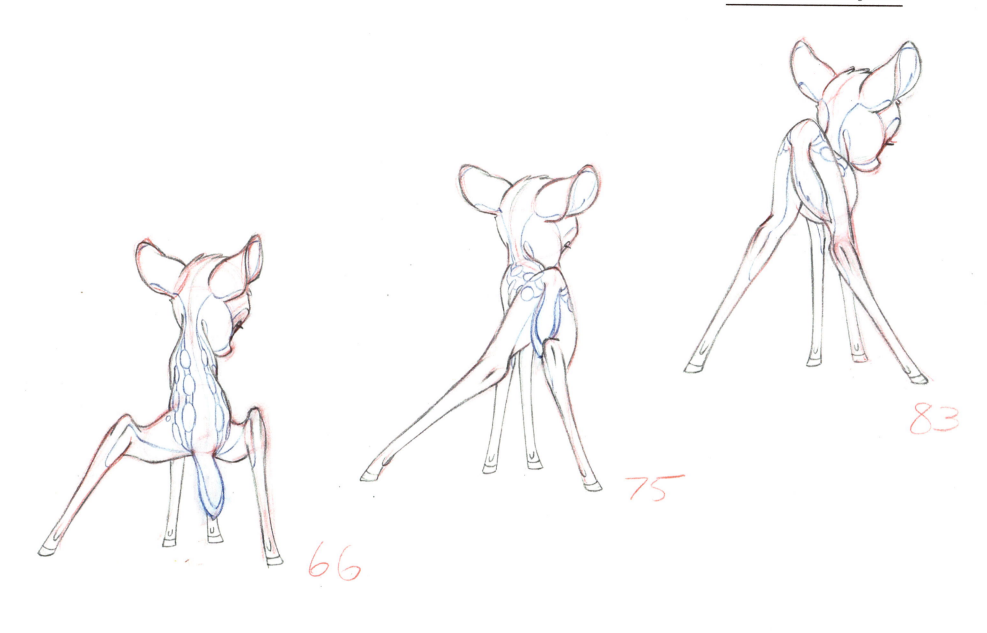

66

75

83

One of Ollie's most charming scenes featuring Thumper, the rabbit, is when he suggests to Bambi that clover's green leaves are really awful to eat. He knows his mother is watching, so he lowers his voice as he talks into Bambi's ear. In this scene he is telling a secret to a friend in a typical childlike manner. Ollie enjoyed animating this type of sincere and entertaining character moment, unlike the upcoming assignments he would soon receive.

Telling Bambi a secret.
© *Disney*

The training and propaganda films produced during the war years were not much fun to work on, according to Ollie. But he did enjoy taking on the two leading ladies in the 1943 short *Reason and Emotion*. These characters live inside the head of a young woman, and they represent opposing sensibilities of her psyche. Their design is a far cry from the realism of *Bambi*, as these two are cartoony types, with potential for expressive animation. Ollie took full advantage of this assignment and brought the characters to life with a lot of guts. Reason is the conservative type, always proper and well-mannered. On the other hand, Emotion is impulsive and fun-loving, but irrational. The story offered rich situations for these two female opponents to disagree and fight with each other.

Ollie explores staging and contrasting attitudes for the female characters in Reason and Emotion. © *Disney*

257

After the end of WWII, Disney got back to theatrical features with the 1946 musical film *Make Mine Music*. One of the short films included was based on Sergei Prokofiev's composition *Peter and the Wolf*. For this section, the Disney artists drew character designs that are round and cartoony, yet the way they move displays a great deal of subtlety. You can see in Ollie's animation of Peter and his Grandpa a careful balance of broad movement and delicate acting. When Peter is caught leaving the house in pursuit of the Wolf, Grandpa's hand grabs the kid in a forceful move and carries him back inside. The forest is dangerous; kids have no business going on a hunt.

After Grandpa dozes off, Peter very warily approaches the old man and reclaims his toy gun from under his heavy arms. These movements are handled with believable posing and timing: a real kid trying to outsmart his grandfather.

Johnston finds the right staging for Peter and Grandpa in this layout sketch.
© *Disney*

258

The film *Song of the South* gave Ollie plenty of opportunities to act out his characters in the broadest way possible. Dialogue scenes with Brer Bear, Brer Rabbit, and Brer Fox required razor-sharp timing. The key poses needed to read very clearly, because they were usually held for a brief moment, until a new thought process led the character to move into a different direction.

Ollie animated the argument between the fast-talking Fox and the massive Bear over who is going to enjoy Brer Rabbit for dinner.

Having been typecast in the past on adorable-type characters, Ollie proved on *Song of the South* that he was perfectly capable of zany, eccentric character animation.

Brer Fox proved Ollie could
handle more eccentric animation.
© *Disney*

259

The short film *Johnny Appleseed* from the 1948 feature *Melody Time* turned out to be a much less enjoyable assignment than the exuberant characters in *Song of the South*. Ollie recollected years later that Johnny didn't have a strong range of emotions: "He never got mad, never showed any deep feelings about anything." Nevertheless Ollie did beautiful scenes with the character at the beginning of the short film, picking apples while singing a song. His movements are based on realistic actions, but there is a light cartoony touch as well. Whenever Johnny jumps, he stays up in the air for a few frames longer than a real person would, before landing on the ground. This kind of timing adds a bit of elegance as well as fantasy to the scene.

Ollie got the chance to show his talent for comedic timing in the *Sleepy Hollow* section of *The Adventures of Ichabod and Mr. Toad*. The antagonist Brom Bones is furious with jealousy when Katrina starts to flirt with Ichabod. He waits outside her house, ready for a confrontation with the schoolmaster. As Ichabod exits, he saves himself by taking advantage of the double door situation.

Johnny stays in the air just a beat longer than is realistic, adding elegance to the scene.
© *Disney*

260

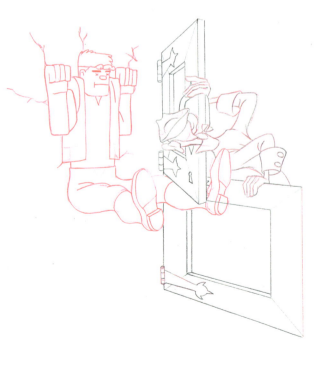

After producing several features that were comprised of individual short films, Disney returned to full-length feature story telling with *Cinderella*. The principal human characters like Cinderella, Lady Tremaine, and Prince Charming were handled very realistically, while the King and the Grand Duke turned out to be cartoony types. The stepsisters Drizella and Anastasia fall somewhere in-between. Ollie Johnston enjoyed developing these two comedic villains. They are extremely spoiled by their mother and take every opportunity to make Cinderella's life a daily hell. Their appearance is more on the humorous side; Ollie refrained from drawing them as truly ugly, grotesque types, he preferred to play up their funny antics. One scene, however, was an exception. Toward the end of the film, Lady Tremaine (the stepmother) presents her two daughters to the Duke. After an awkward curtsey, Anastasia remarks: "Your grace." In this close-up scene Ollie tried purposely to portray her as ugly as possible, so that the Duke would react in a repulsed manner. When Walt Disney saw the scene in pencil form, he told Ollie: "You might want to pull that expression back a little, she looks hideous." The corrected scene still shows a very unattractive Anastasia.

Making Anastasia as ugly as possible.
© *Disney*

Not only does Ollie play up the comedy in Ichabod's animation, but the much more realistic Brom Bones goes through a hysterical routine as well.
© *Disney*

261

In 1952 Disney released a charming short film called *Susie, the Little Blue Coupe*. The story was developed by Bill Peet and it deals with the ups and downs in the life of an automobile. It wasn't the first time Disney turned modes of transportation into successful animated personalities—the train Casey Jr. in *Dumbo* and the plane Pedro in *Saludos Amigos* were living, breathing machines. But Susie was the first "thinking" automobile, a true challenge for any animator. Ollie Johnston found clever ways to humanize certain auto parts. The windshield became the eyes, the hood was turned into a nose, and the wheels assume functions of arms and legs. The audience completely identifies with this humanized vehicle, because of the character's sincere emotions. Susie adores her new owner at the start of the film, but she is heartbroken at a later age, when being discarded onto a second-hand lot and eventually to a junkyard. The animator's challenge was to inject human emotions into a machine and make it look entertaining. Ollie animated Susie's body with surprising elasticity even though it is supposed to be made of metal. One of animation's most lovable inanimate objects.

Susie was animation's first
"thinking" automobile.
© *Disney*

262

Working on the title character of the film *Alice in Wonderland* meant a shift for Ollie Johnston from broad animated types like Susie to a more finessed and realistic style of animation. Live-action reference was filmed to provide a basis for the animators' work. Ollie found this method somewhat restrictive because the main acting choices were made by actress Kathryn Beaumont. But there were scenes that did call for the animator's imagination. Ollie drew Alice meeting the talking doorknob, who encourages her to drink out of a particular bottle in order to change her size. Only then would she be able to pass through the tiny door. Early attempts fail and Alice becomes increasingly frustrated. Emotions like these on a realistic character needed to be carefully drawn and timed. Ollie pointed out years later that animating Alice wasn't one of his favorite assignments, but that he learned a lot from working with live action. "It teaches you about subtlety," he said.

Although Ollie found working with live-action reference challenging, he admitted that he learnt a lot from the experience.
© *Disney*

263

Ollie also animated the more caricatured King of Hearts, who turned out to be a much easier assignment. Broadly designed as a tiny character and in stark contrast to his mountainous wife, the Queen of Hearts, Ollie gave the King a unique way of running. His feet are not drawn at all, instead the lower end of his coat propels him to move forward. It is a nonsensical, fun type of motion.

But it was Ollie's animation of Alice that impressed Walt Disney, so naturally he offered him the part of Wendy in the upcoming production of *Peter Pan*. Sensing Ollie's frustration, Walt changed his mind and handed him Smee, Captain Hook's pirate sidekick. This character assignment led to one of the funniest, appealing and most interesting cartoon creations ever created. Smee is basically a nice guy who feels the need to act mean only because his boss is the villainous Captain Hook. He even apologizes to Tinker Bell for capturing her so that Hook can interrogate the pixie. Smee often acts uneasy and is intimidated by the Captain. Ollie Johnston animated him with hilarious nervous gestures and attitudes. At one point in the film, Smee offers Hook a shave. Unbeknown to him, he ends up shaving the back side of a seagull instead.

Sheer disbelief and panic overcomes him when he find's Hook's head gone. "I never shaved him this close before!" His hands quiver as he feels through the wet towel searching for the missing scalp. He grabs the top of his hat and shakes it, not knowing what to do next. This is an extremely funny performance, full of inventive and surprising gestures.

Ollie ended up drawing most scenes with Smee, a character who ranks among his best animated efforts. Comic timing and brilliant acting choices make him stand out as a Disney sidekick who works for a villain but comes across as a likeable and entertaining type.

Smee is one of Ollie's most entertaining creations.
© Disney

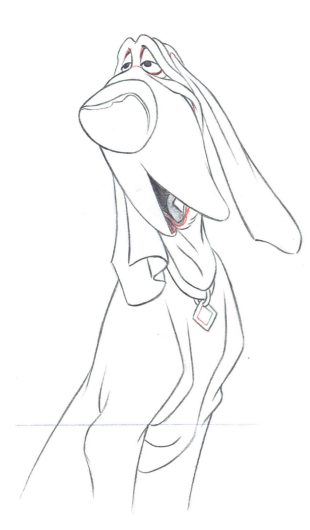

The dog characters in *Lady and the Tramp* required the kind of realistic approach in terms of their movements not seen since *Bambi*. These canines needed to walk and run with real weight. *Lady and the Tramp* is a sincere love story, making simple cartoony designs out of place.

Ollie did scenes with most of the dogs, including Tramp and Lady. One of his favorite dogs turned out to be Trusty, the old bloodhound. Ollie sympathized with this warm, grandfatherly type, who had lost his sense of smell. Trusty's very loose skin gave the animators the opportunity to show these folds in overlapping actions, particularly in dialogue scenes. Ollie applied strong squash and stretch to Trusty's face which not only adds age, but it is simply fun to watch.

Trusty, the old bloodhound who has lost his sense of smell.
© *Disney*

265

For the production of *Sleeping Beauty*, Walt assigned specific characters to certain animators. For the most part that animator would be responsible for that character only. An exception was the three fairies, who often were portrayed as one unit. Flora, Fauna, and Merryweather stand firm against Maleficent, help raise Aurora in the forest, and the happy ending is largely their work. But their personalities do differ from one another, which made them interesting and fun to work with. Ollie and his colleague Frank Thomas animated all of the fairies' important acting scenes. With all three of them often appearing in the same scene together, staging and composition became an interesting challenge. Clear silhouettes in their poses were very important, so that the group image did not become confusing to an audience. Luckily the widescreen format provided ample space to place these three ladies in.

Flora and Fauna gently encourage Merryweather to give her gift.
© Disney

266

Ollie observes the anatomy and motion of real Dalmatians.
© *Disney*

The film *One Hundred and One Dalmatians* was groundbreaking for its sketchy look and modern art direction , but characters like Pongo and Perdita still needed to be animated the old-fashioned way. The routine of bringing Disney characters to life with drawings on sheets of paper had not changed at all. The animators started out by studying real Dalmatians before caricaturing them for animation.

A rough concept sketch for the moment when Pongo faces Cruella De Vil for the first time.
© *Disney*

267

At the beginning of the film, Ollie animated Pongo's decision to pursue a young lady with her female Dalmatian, who had just passed by the house. He tricks his master Roger Radcliff into believing that it is time for a walk by changing the time on a clock. There is a strong sense of determination to catch up with the two ladies. Pongo pulls Roger along with all his might, until he finally spots them on a park bench.

A few key scenes involving the character of Nanny in *One Hundred and One Dalmatians* were also animated by Ollie. Visually she comes across as a possible relative of *Sleeping Beauty*'s three fairies.

Pongo straining to catch up with Anita and Perdita.
© Disney

Nanny is similar in style to Merryweather from Sleeping Beauty.
© Disney

The Sword in the Stone continued the sketchy visual style that was introduced with *One Hundred and One Dalmatians*. Walt Disney had been critical of this "unfinished looking" approach to his animated films, but most animators enjoyed seeing their own pencil drawings move on the screen (instead of inked tracings). Ollie had a lot to do with developing the relationship of three of the main characters, Merlin, Wart, and Archimedes, the owl. They present an interesting dynamic. Merlin puts it upon himself to give young Wart a real education. Even though he does not succeed very well in this endeavor, the boy is in awe of the wizard. Archimedes is actually the smartest of them all and criticizes Merlin's efforts frequently. Ollie animated most of the opening sequence of the film, when we first see Merlin as he is having trouble getting water out of a well. Eventually Wart appears as he literally falls through the roof of Merlin's house, just in time for tea.

Even though Ollie enjoyed working on characters like Wart and Merlin, he thought that their relationship never reached the kind of depth you would feel with Mowgli and Baloo from *The Jungle Book*, the animated feature that followed *The Sword in the Stone*.

Wart and Merlin from The Sword in the Stone.
© *Disney*

269

A penguin waiter from Mary Poppins.
© *Disney*

In-between those two pictures, the animators were asked to animate characters that interacted with human actors. In the classic film *Mary Poppins*, Julie Andrews and Dick Van Dyke share the screen with cartoon farm animals, racehorses, and four cheerful penguins. Ollie Johnston animated these arctic birds as busy waiters, eager to serve Mary Poppins. The penguins' movements as a group needed to be choreographed carefully, their hectic but enthusiastic actions would otherwise come off as confusing to watch.

The Jungle Book is a unique Disney film, its story was kept extremely simple so that the characters would have plenty of time to interact with each other. Walt Disney knew that the entertainment needed to come from the animal characters' performances, which left the animators with more responsibility than usual. Previous Disney films had been much more story-driven, but *The Jungle Book* relied completely on strong character animation. The studio at that time had a small but powerful animation unit that could deliver performances of the highest level. For the most part, animators were handed out complete sequences to animate, no matter how many characters were involved. That type of casting resulted in a situation where different animators worked on the same personalities. It gave them the chance to not only develop individual characters, but complex relationships as well.

Ollie Johnston focused on Baloo and Mowgli, and he also animated scenes with Bagheera and the Girl at the end of the movie. Baloo's introduction in the film is one of Ollie's masterpieces. The bear's carefree nature is immediately established by his on-screen singing and "dance walking."

Those moves look completely natural and even improvised, yet a scene like this one requires a lot of analysis and careful planning from the animator. The character's weight shifts constantly, arms and legs have separate unique moving patterns, and the action is synchronized to a musical beat. This complex kind of motion means that all drawings are done by the animator, there are no in-betweens. Every position is unique and important. Ollie recalled that Walt Disney himself had acted out Baloo's steps one day in the hallway of the studio. That little performance by Ollie's boss became the foundation for the personality of the bear.

FACING PAGE
Baloo's dance walk was inspired by a demonstration given by Walk Disney.
© *Disney*

271

Ollie Johnston again developed some of the principal characters for the film *The Aristocats*. For most of his life, Ollie had been a dog-owner, and a lot of research for his canine animated characters was done right at home. But when he started to work on Duchess, the mother cat, and her three little ones, he proved that he had an affinity for felines as well. The kittens Marie, Toulouse, and Berlioz are effectively based on real children. As one would expect, the two brothers gang up on their sister often, and when things go wrong the familiar blaming game ensues. Their personalities come through during a music lesson and when Toulouse paints a portrait of Edgar, the butler. Their behavior and attitudes are sincere and childlike.

Although a dog-owner, The Aristocats *proved that Ollie also had an affinity for felines.*
© Disney

Ollie also animated scenes with Amelia and Abigail Gabble, a couple of English geese who giggle constantly. Watching them on the screen, many in the audience probably remember an aunt or two with similar character traits.

While these geese needed to move in a naturalistic way, Prince John from the film *Robin Hood* had to act much more human-like—after all, he was an anthropomorphic lion. His sidekick Sir Hiss might slither like a real snake, but he is also able to get into human-like poses by using his tail as a hand. Ollie saw the potential for rich personality material, and he created tour de force performances with these two comedic villains. Their facial expressions are based on the actors who provided their voices. Peter Ustinov is Prince John, a cowardly lion, and Terry-Thomas is Sir Hiss, a sniveling snake. The film's story might not come up to classic Disney standards, but as far as character relationships go, this is one of the most entertaining. Prince John seeks constant confirmation for being a good monarch and when Sir Hiss doesn't comply, physical punishment follows. Nevertheless, Hiss is committed to pleasing his boss, which makes him a partner in crime. It was important that Ollie handled both characters. If another animator had drawn Sir Hiss, for example, their interactions would not have been as seamless. When Prince John acted aggressively, Ollie knew immediately how the snake would have to react.

Ollie captures the uneasy relationship between two comic villains.
© *Disney*

273

The orphan Penny from The Rescuers.
© *Disney*

For the film *The Rescuers*, Ollie was assigned to several characters. He supervised the animation of the orphan girl Penny and Rufus, the old cat. He also developed the personality of Orville, the albatross who runs his own airline. Several important acting scenes featuring the mice Bernard and Bianca were also drawn by Ollie. This is very diverse group of characters, from sentimental and comic to leading types. It is fair to say that Ollie carried a large part of this picture with quality animation, but also quantity. His most important contribution was arguably developing Penny into a character the audience would feel for. This is a girl who is sad for most of the film, not necessarily an appealing attitude to watch for long. But the way Ollie expressed her inner feelings to Rufus reveals that she still holds a glimmer of hope to be adopted one day, and that makes her sympathetic and appealing.

Ollie's farewell animation assignment was for the 1981 film *The Fox and the Hound*. At that time Disney's veteran master animators had taken on a second role as teachers to a new generation of animators. Ollie lectured and gave advice to several newcomers to the studio, including Tim Burton and Glen Keane. But he still found the time to animate one sequence. Tod, the fox meets Vixey in the forest, and his attempts to impress her result in some awkward, but funny moments.

Both Ollie and his colleague Frank Thomas stated that they did not feel challenged working on *The Fox and the Hound*. The story material and the character concepts were too familiar and reminded them of previous films they had worked on. It was time to put down the pencil and pursue new interests. For the next few years Ollie and Frank wrote a number of important books on character animation and Disney philosophy in general.

Looking over some of Ollie Johnston's drawings, there is a lot to admire. A special appeal can be seen in all of them, whether it is a hero or a villain we are looking at. Ollie never forgot what he had learned from his mentor Fred Moore, that charm is an important ingredient in depicting a character. Without it, the audience might lose interest.

It is also interesting to observe Ollie's light touch with pencil and paper. It seems like he never got frustrated during the animation process. Just a few careful construction lines with delicate pencil strokes on top. This meant that he spent little time on one given drawing, he quickly moved on to the next ones. Ollie Johnston was not only one of Disney's best animators, on many film productions he was also the fastest. What an astounding talent!

Ollie's final animation assignment was The Fox and the Hound.
© Disney

275

*P*inocchio

1940
PINOCCHIO
ROUGH ANIMATION
Seq. 4.9, Sc. 21

These beautiful drawings define Pinocchio's emotions sensitively and with great insight. The Blue Fairy has reappeared and is wondering why he didn't go to school.

Being locked up in a cage Pinocchio feels embarrassed to face the Fairy. "I was going to school… 'til I met somebody." During the first part of his statement he looks concerned; he doesn't quite know what to tell her. But, the fact that he met somebody is actually the truth, and his expression changes to a smile. For a second he is proud of himself and his explanation, so far so good. But moments later he changes his angle and reports that he ran into two big monsters with big green eyes. Perhaps a little lie will get him out of this interrogation.

Ollie found the perfect uneasy gesture to visualize the dialogue. Pinocchio uses a finger to twirl one side of his shorts. Ollie emphasizes the word *met*, as Pinocchio leans forward showing a hint of confidence in what he just said.

© *Disney*

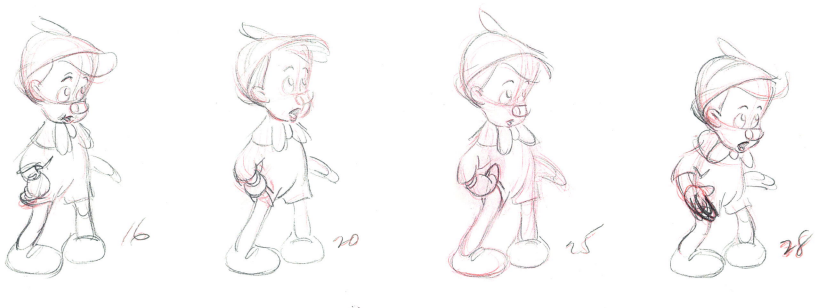

Alice in Wonderland

1951
ALICE
ROUGH ANIMATION
Seq. 3, Sc. 22

Alice has gone through a lot in an effort to try and pass through a miniature door. When she reduces her size hoping she would be able to pass through, the doorknob informs her that he is locked. Ollie animated Alice's frustrated reaction during her encounter with this strange character from Wonderland. In this close-up scene she slides her right hand up her face in an attitude of disappointment and annoyance. During this action Alice's nose is affected by being flattened for a short moment. It is an effective way to show a soft part of her face reacting to the touch of the firm palm of her hand. This gives the illusion that the audience is watching a flesh and blood character on the screen. A subtle contact like this one makes a big difference in making a series of drawings come alive.

© *Disney*

278

Peter Pan

1953
SMEE
ROUGH ANIMATION
Seq. 11, Sc. 6

As Captain Hook declares to Tinker Bell that he intends to leave the island, Mr. Smee reacts surprised, but delighted. It was his wish all along to sail away and forget Peter Pan. "I'm glad you agree, Cap'n [hic], I'll tell the crew."

Smee quickly hides the bottle he was enjoying inside the piano and shows his excitement through a clapping gesture. A hilarious little hiccup follows, before he leaves the scene with the intention to inform the ship's crew.

Ollie's acting choices reveal Smee's misunderstanding of the situation, which is right in character.

Judging from the hasty way Smee disposes of the bottle tells us that he feels guilty drinking the wine in the first place. During the mid-sentence hiccup, his startled expression is supported by the stretch of his hat. In anticipation of his exit, Smee takes a couple of steps backward to gain some momentum. This is a beautifully textured and choreographed scene.

© Disney

282

22

26

29

31

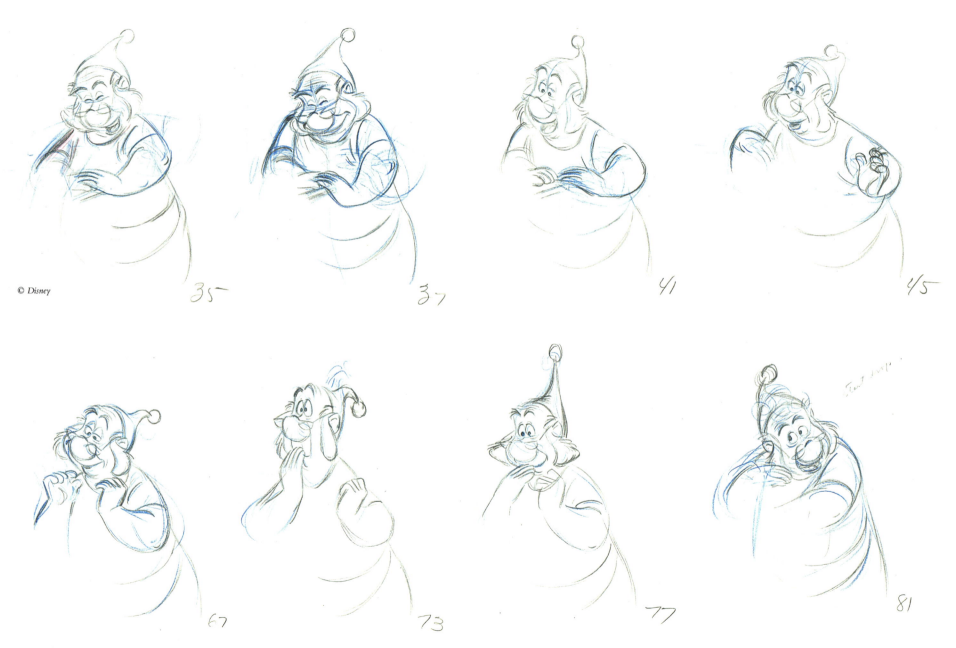

284

53

55

59

63

85

73

99

107

Lady and the Tramp

1955
TRUSTY
ROUGH ANIMATION
Seq. 11, Sc. 17

After the embarrassing dog pound episode, Trusty and Jock pay a visit to Lady, who is now confined to a doghouse. When Tramp suddenly arrives he is being met with contempt and disregard. It is clear that Lady is not the least interested in seeing him.

Trusty offers support by telling her: "If this pussin is annoying you, Miss Lady…" Followed by Trusty: "…we'll gladly throw the rascal out!"

Trusty's expression is full of disdain as he says the line of dialogue over his shoulder.

Every one of his mouth shapes communicates that emotion very clearly. Since this is an old bloodhound with an extremely soft muzzle configuration, Ollie could take full advantage of this elasticity. Strong squash and stretch is applied here, as well as caricatured mouth shapes. As Trusty turns around, the motion of his long ears supports the head move nicely.

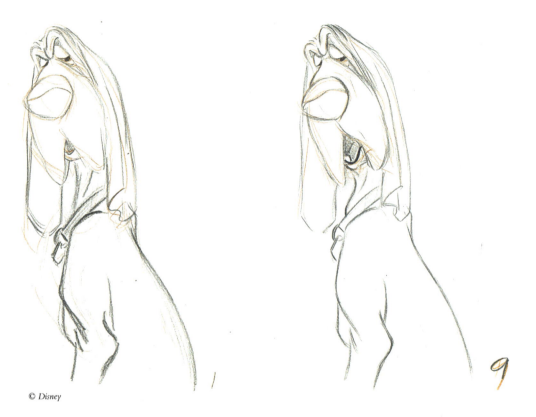

© *Disney*

286

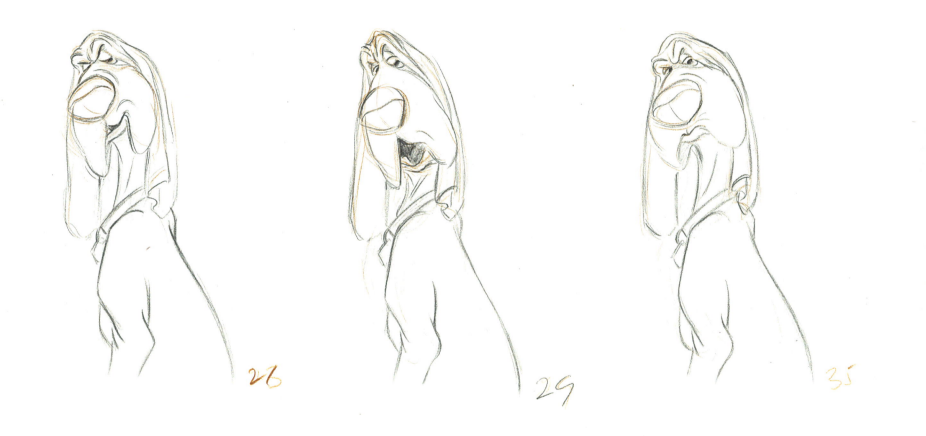

39

© Disney

55

63

87

The Jungle Book

1967
BALOO
CLEAN-UP ANIMATION
Seq. 4, Sc. 126

During the "Bare Necessities" song number, Baloo interrupts his dancing for a moment in order to create a jungle sandwich, made up of leaves and fruit. He advises Mowgli: "Don't pick up the prickly pear by the paw, when you pick a pear, try to use the claw."

Like everything Baloo does, there is entertainment and showmanship in preparing this exotic snack. When both of his claws hold enough food, he arranges the chunks of fruit as if they are playing cards. By mixing and combining them, one tall eatable tower emerges, which the bear quickly devours with great ease.

All of these pieces of action are highly unrealistic and even illogical. Yet Ollie's animation looks completely natural and believable. Any of the key poses are drawn within a clear silhouette, which makes it easy for the viewer to follow the fruit pile's path of action, from being picked to entering Baloo's open mouth.

© Disney

52

59

67

© Disney

106

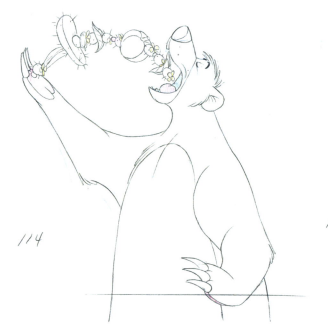

114

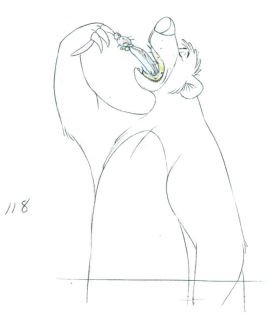

118

73

86

89

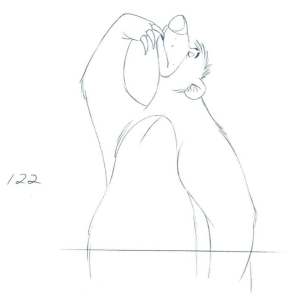

122

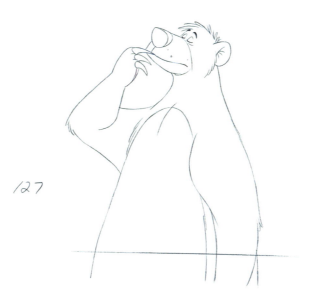

127

130

John Lounsbery

When Eric Larson screened the opening sequence from *Peter Pan* for students in his training program in early 1982, a particular scene caused quite a discussion afterwards. After George Darling unsuccessfully tried to get his children's attention, he jumps from a seated position high up in the air and onto his feet, before ordering that Nana, the dog, be taken outside where she would spend the nights from now on. It is an unusual and surprisingly broad piece of animation for a character who needed to come across as a believable father to the Darling children, Wendy, John, and Michael. Some of the young animators in the audience that day felt that the jump looked too cartoony, as it reminded them of the type of action Donald Duck would perform. Others thought that the scene greatly enhanced the father's emotional and extraverted personality. The person who animated George Darling was John Lounsbery, a much-respected artist who was known as a reserved and humble man. Many of his animated characters had eccentric, lively, over-the-top temperaments. They ranged from colorful villains to broad comedic types. John was one of the top draftsmen at the studio, who could adapt to any design style that was required for a particular film. His lines on paper had an energetic quality that expressed how strongly he felt about the characters' emotions. He was also a patient teacher who took time to go over the work of young animators who often sought his advice and expertise. John often redrew their poses to strengthen the silhouette, or retimed a scene to make it come alive. Many newcomers to the studio would not dare to present a drawing to the unpredictable Milt Kahl, but they knew that John Lounsbery in his quiet way always gave productive advice. Because of his unfortunate early passing in 1976 this underrated, self-deprecating artist never experienced the kind of fame that Walt Disney's animators encountered after books about their legacy were published, and when documentary films pointed out the men behind the Disney magic. John got hired by Disney in 1935, when the studio was gearing up to produce the enormously ambitious film *Snow White and the Seven Dwarfs*. He soon was chosen to assist established animator Norm Ferguson with his animation. "Fergy," as he was called by his colleagues, had become an expert on animating Mickey Mouse's dog Pluto.

In the 1934 short film *Playful Pluto*, Fergy animated the dog trying to free himself from sticky flypaper. At a certain point, Pluto looks directly into camera, allowing the audience to participate in his thought process and decision-making. These animated drawings showed the character thinking, before he took action trying to rid himself of the gluey pest. The scene was an important example to younger animators for proving that mere action wasn't enough to bring a personality to life; the character had to think in order to become believable to an audience. Fergy animated the scary Witch in the feature *Snow White*, and Lounsbery studied those scenes carefully as he was doing assistant work on them. After a while, Fergy felt it was time for his student take on his own piece of animation. He handed Lounsbery the scene in which the old Hag goes down a trap door as she cackles gleefully, "Buried alive," in anticipation of her evil plan to kill Snow White. This wasn't an easy scene to animate. There is the main downward action, she is addressing her dialogue to the left-behind raven, and her laugh makes her body shiver. This affects the motion of her left arm, which is holding the trap door. Those parts needed to move erratically to complement the Witch's laugh.

A couple of key drawings show the potential in young John Lounsbery as an animator.
© Disney

FACE ALL
IN D.X. SHADOW
EXCEPT EYES
FROM
HERE TO
END OF SCENE

297

After *Snow White* was completed, John got the chance to animate Pluto in short films such as *Society Dog Show* and *The Pointer*. At that time Fergy still supervised those scenes and subsequently influenced the young animator. Lounsbery's use of strong squash and stretch within loose, bold action was a direct result of his mentor's tutoring. The two men worked very well together, and by the time production began on *Pinocchio*, Fergy requested that Lounsbery join the unit that would animate the fox, Honest John, and his partner in crime, the cat Gideon.

Ferguson himself did not animate on the film, instead he served as one of four sequence directors. In this new capacity he helped shape the story material for these two villains.

Several animators were responsible for animating the fox and the cat throughout the film, but Lounsbery drew their introductory scenes. As Pinocchio hops along on his way to school, he catches the eye of Honest John, who is astonished at what he sees: "Look Giddy, look! It's amazing, a live puppet without strings."

Honest John and Gideon have their eyes set on Pinocchio.
© *Disney*

These two crafty, contrasting characters needed to perform with theatrical showmanship. Often the fox becomes an actor as he tries to persuade Pinocchio to forget about school and join show business instead. He is trying to be convincing, and his poses are grand and over the top. The cat usually agrees with whatever the fox is saying, even though more often than not Gideon doesn't have a clue what's going on. As they interact with Pinocchio they form an irresistible trio, and the most bewildered misunderstandings become highly entertaining. When working with campy, exaggerated poses, it is of utmost importance that they read clearly to the viewer. The essence of a thought or mood must be found, which always requires a good silhouette within a pose. The way the character gets in and out of such a pose becomes an important factor for a successful performance as well. Usually the timing between held poses is quick and smooth. Lounsbery had learned these principles from studying Fergy's work and applied that knowledge to great advantage. As far as good draftsmanship was concerned, he would soon surpass his mentor.

Fergy and Lounsbery worked together again on *Fantasia*'s "Dance of the Hours" section. Ferguson co-directed the sequence, and John was put in charge of developing the personality of Ben Ali Gator, who becomes love-struck with his dance partner, Hyacinth Hippo. This hilarious relationship offered a number of truly memorable character moments. There are 12 ballet-dancing alligators, but only Ben Ali stands out as a definitive personality. As the gators surround the sleeping hippo, he shows up late, way up high on the columns. Lounsbery animated his entrance with a silly walk, followed by a fluster of arm gestures as he discovers the sleeping "beauty" below. From that moment on nothing can stop him from pursuing the object of his affection. His eyes flutter in adoration, and he places his hands over his heart. Hyacinth awakens and takes off, but her body language says "Come and get me!" After a hilarious *pas de deux*, an energetic chase ensues, and eventually the other gators, hippos, and other animals get involved.

Lounsbery animated Ben Ali as a professional dancer. Gone are the goofy moves from his early scenes, for the rest of the sequence he dances with style and grace. His relatively skinny body bends and turns in the most unexpected ways, but always ending up in a flamboyant, theatrical pose. This is the work of a star animator, who impresses with technical expertise, musicality, and outstanding draftsmanship. Lounsbery stated in an interview how much he enjoyed getting all the gator's dance business across, in sync to the beat of Ponchielli's music.

*Ben Ali Gator has all the style of
a professional dancer.*
© *Disney*

301

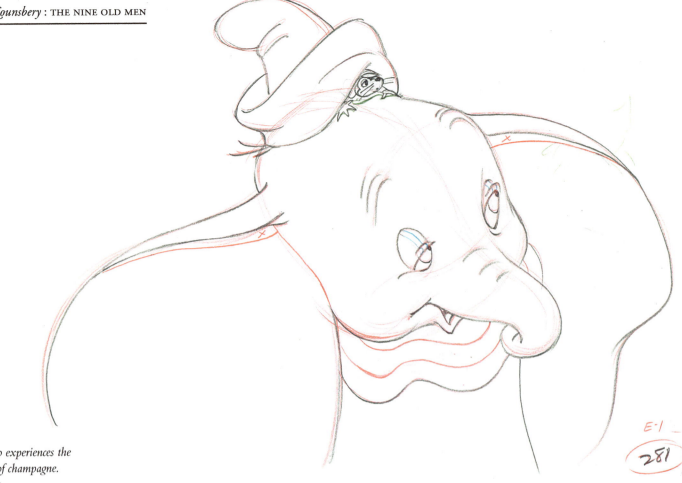

*Dumbo experiences the
effects of champagne.*
© Disney

Every great animator has a range; he is able to take on a number of different character assignments. Lounsbery had shown that he had a feel for exaggerated, vaudevillian types, but his next role would demand a whole different set of emotions. John was promoted to supervising animator on the movie *Dumbo*, where he ended up working on the title character, along with several other animators. One of the sections he worked on takes place after Timothy, the mouse, and Dumbo return from a visit to Dumbo's imprisoned mother. The little elephant's walk feels heavy, and a few tears are rolling down his cheeks. Timothy tries to cheer up his friend, who so unjustly got separated from his mother. Suddenly Dumbo gets the hiccups. These beautifully animated bursts add some lighthearted comedy in this overall sad situation. With each hiccup, Dumbo's head jolts abruptly while his trunk and large ears are animated in overlapping action. But it is the expressions Lounsbery draws that make these scenes so charming. Dumbo's eyes open wide in surprise before settling. Timothy suggests that drinking some water will help the elephant's condition, but by accident Dumbo ends up sipping champagne instead. The hiccups continue, and his expressions become more and more hilarious. Lounsbery injects so much appeal into these scenes; as a matter of fact, he probably drew the character better and with more charm than the rest of the animators. As the story continues, Dumbo starts producing large champagne bubbles, which leads into the famous "Pink Elephants on Parade" sequence.

Like most animators at Disney, during the Second World War, John Lounsbery was cast on propaganda films like *Victory through Air Power* and *Chicken Little*. The postwar feature *Make Mine Music* included the short film *Peter and the Wolf*. John was in charge of developing the frightening Wolf. The character's appearance is cartoony, as is the rest of the cast, but there is no doubt that this is a vicious creature, who presents a great danger to Peter and his friends. Some of the Wolf's close-ups are very effective in showing this villain's bad intentions.

Enormous teeth and drooling saliva enhance the Wolf's horrifying personality.
© Disney

The animal characters in *Song of the South* were played for comedy, even though Brer Fox and Brer Bear could be a threat to little Brer Rabbit. Like everybody involved with this film, John enjoyed working with these eccentric characters very much. Among other scenes, he animated the section following the capture of Brer Rabbit in a sapling trap. The bear comes along and inquires about the nature of this odd situation, when the clever rabbit convinces him to take his place as a kind of a scarecrow. The contrast between these personalities offered John unique ways of timing the characters' acting patterns. The rabbit is quick and energetic, while the bear moves very slowly.

Brer Rabbit persuades
Brer Bear to take on his job.
© Disney

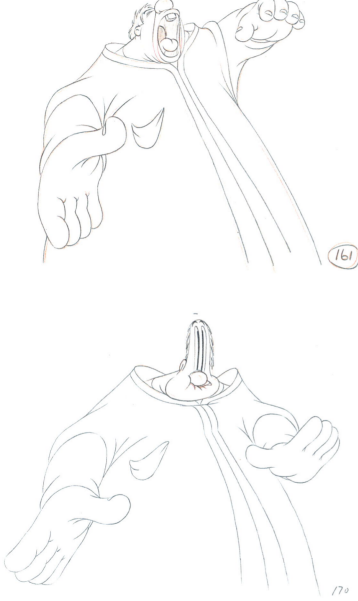

John's next character required startling and unexpected type of movements. Willie the Giant is the villain in the *Mickey and the Beanstalk* section from the feature *Fun and Fancy Free*. He has magical powers that allow him to turn himself into any type of creature. During his opening song he comes across as a jolly, almost likeable giant, until he discovers Mickey, Donald, and Goofy. He locks them up in a box, except Mickey, who narrowly escapes, but only to find himself trapped in the Giant's shirt pocket next to an oversized snuff-box. In reaction to the snuff, Mickey can't help but sneeze out loud. The tobacco reaches the Giant's nose, and he immediately reacts with several abrupt inhales. Just when the audience anticipates a giant size sneeze, John instead animates the silliest reaction. Willie's face goes through a couple of quick distortions as we hear a funny, little twang. The scene always gets a big laugh from the audience, because no giant is supposed to sneeze like this.

A not so giant-size sneeze from Willie.
© Disney

305

After *Fun and Fancy Free*, Walt Disney was not quite ready yet to restart producing feature-length films, the war had severely interrupted the studio's flow of income. Instead a few more so-called package films followed. These full-length movies each contained a number of short subjects, which were fairly inexpensive to make. John worked on several scenes for *Melody Time* and *The Adventures of Ichabod and Mr. Toad*, before joining the team of animators that would finally re-establish the full-length Disney animated feature film with the story of *Cinderella*. The film's cast of characters ranged from realistic to cartoony in concept and design. Lounsbery steered away from subtle human personalities; instead he animated a number of broad, expressive characters. When the mice Jaq and Gus try to locate clothing items that would be useful for creating a party dress for Cinderella, they run into Lucifer, who is asleep on a footstool. An outrageous sequence begins in which they outwit the cat repeatedly, and sneak a roll of fabric and a bead necklace by the evil feline. This section of the film was directed by Wilfred Jackson, who worked very closely with John on the timing and the suspense of certain moments. The audience is led to believe that eventually the cat, who is not stupid, will outsmart and catch the mice, but instead Jaq and Gus do succeed, barely. The animation is flawless. The quick, erratic movements of the mice are contrasted by the heavy, slow-moving cat, who only commits to a chase when he believes the mice are within his reach.

Jaq and Gus need to outsmart Lucifer in order to collect clothing items for Cinderella's dress.
© Disney

Lounsbery
was also respon-
sible for trans-
forming a horse into
a coachman and a dog
into a footman during the
Fairy Godmother sequence.
Each animal is magically lifted in
the air; they bounce exactly three times,
in sync with the lyrics, "bibbidi, bobbidi, boo,"
before taking on their human form. These musical and visual
rhythms, combined with stunning special effects, give the scene extraordinary beauty.

Bruno, the dog and Major, the horse begin their magical transformation.
© Disney

307

John Lounsbery continued animating non-realistic characters for the film *Alice in Wonderland*, where zany, oddball types could be found in abundance. He joined a small team of artists who brought the smoking Caterpillar to life. It was John who animated the famous line when he encounters Alice: "Who are you?" With each exhale the smoke forms a letter, in this case: O, R, and U. Lounsbery anticipates each mouth shape very effectively. For example, before his mouth forms an "O" for the word "who" his lips are relaxed, then come forward to illustrate that sound. This makes for smooth and convincing dialogue animation.

"Who are you?"
© *Disney*

Ward Kimball had started work on the Mad Tea Party sequence, but he needed help to finish it. John took on a number of scenes featuring the Mad Hatter. They turned out to look and feel indistinguishable from Kimball's version of that character. Zany, unpredictable acting came easy to Lounsbery and Kimball couldn't have found a better collaborator.

Another character John animated for the film turned out to be more subtle but equally fantastical. The Red Rose conducted a choir of flowers performing the song "All in the Golden Afternoon." She turned out to be more sympathetic toward Alice and interacted with her without hostility. To bring a flower to life with human characteristics probably sounds like a difficult assignment, but her design already suggested a definite female type. A friendly human face was drawn in the center of the blossom, and twigs and leafs made up her arms and dress. Still, this rose needed to move in a restricted manner. The audience should never assume that she would be able to take a few steps and walk like a human. Motion is limited to her upper body only.

The Mad Hatter explains to Alice what an unbirthday is.
© Disney

The friendly and sympathetic Red Rose.
© Disney

309

Disney's next film, *Peter Pan*, had an almost all-human cast, with only a few eccentric personalities. One of them was George Darling, a somewhat typical Victorian father who was strict and temperamental, but very much in love with his family. John Lounsbery animated all of his scenes at the beginning of the film. What could have been a secondary character in the hands of a different animator became the comic center of the Darling family. Had he been handled as a realistic, conventional father figure, this family

Because of his outgoing personality, Mr. Darling becomes the most engaging character in this sequence from Peter Pan.
© Disney

would come across as boring to an audience. But because of Mr. Darling's frustrations and emotional outbursts we enjoy watching him as well as his interaction with family members. During his first scene he enters the children's nursery in search of his tuxedo cufflinks. He eventually looks under a bed sheet to instead discover his white shirtfront, with some kind of treasure map drawn all over it. He lifts it up high, expressing horror and disbelief. This is one of many Lounsbery's scenes, which is very dramatically staged, but because of solid draftsmanship, still fits in with the more realistic characters in the sequence.

310

The fact that John also drew scenes with Wendy, Michael, and Captain Hook proves his versatility as an animator. A few wonderful assignments were coming John's way when production began on Disney's first widescreen animated film *Lady and the Tramp*. This wide format presented new challenges, particularly for layout artists and animators. The extended horizontal screen required a much wider representation of environments, while animators needed to fill up the extra space with more characters. In close-up scenes, a single drawing of a dog's head would often look isolated. One or two other dogs needed to be added in order to present a pleasing composition. All this meant more work, but also additional costs.

Walt Disney was very much aware of Lounsbery's comedic strengths, and he cast him on Tony and Joe, two lively Italian-Americans who run the restaurant that became the backdrop for the most romantic scene in animation. Tony is the proprietor, a large figure with big gestures that communicate joy as well as anger. Joe is the chef, who is much smaller in size but equally expressive. One scene in particular became a high point that typifies their relationship. When Tramp shows up at the restaurant's back entrance by himself, Tony orders Joe to bring out some bones for the dog. Then Lady appears from behind a food container. When Joe returns from the kitchen with a bowl of bones, Tony reacts in a volatile manner as he kicks the bowl out of Joe's hands: "What'sa matter for you, Joe… I break'a your face. Tonight'a butch, hes'a getta the best'a in'a house." John Lounsbery felt these personalities. His animation shows the same passion that these two characters display. Tony's wild gesturing comes across as an affectionate satire of Italian articulation. Great acting choices, phenomenal draftsmanship and believable motion make Tony and Joe truly masterfully animated creations. Lounsbery was so attuned to this assignment that he impressed and surprised his fellow animators with his astonishing personality animation.

Tony serenades Lady and Tramp.
© *Disney*

311

John also animated key scenes with the English bulldog Bull, who, along with other dogs, befriends Lady in the dog pound. Bull's facial features are loose and rubbery, which is perfectly appropriate for this type of dog. Every one of his dialogue scenes are a joy to watch, because of unusual mouth configurations, and gutsy overlapping action of cheeks and lips.

Bull's unusual mouth configuration helped to create entertaining dialogue scenes.
© Disney

312

When Lady and Tramp try to visit the local zoo in order to seek help from a beaver, they find a policeman guarding the entrance. Tramp engages a passing professor in a fight with the policeman, so he and Lady can slip into the zoo. Lounsbery animated this spirited sequence, which involved physical interaction, since the two characters fought and argued with one another over the issue who this dog (Tramp) belongs to. Strong use of squash and stretch helped to keep this altercation lively and entertaining.

The professor tries unsuccessfully to convince the policeman that he is not Tramp's owner.
© Disney

313

*King Hubert brandishes an unusual weapon
during his disagreement with King Stefan.*
© *Disney*

The shift in style from *Lady and the Tramp*
to *Sleeping Beauty* was significant in many
ways. Disney characters did not appear as
dimensional figures, instead flat graphic shapes
made up their design. John Lounsbery's drawing style
of King Hubert and King Stefan did not exactly match the
sophisticated look Milt Kahl brought to the sequence in which
both characters toast to the future of their children. But by the
time John's scenes were cleaned up and traced on to cels, the differ-
ences became very minimal. Milt Kahl animated the first half of the
sequence, when both kings lift their glasses in friendship. John takes
over as an argument develops over the possibility that Prince Phillip
and Princess Aurora might not like each other when introduced.
This was smart casting since Kahl excelled at nuanced subtle
performances, while Lounsbery preferred outgoing, extraverted
acting.

John also enjoyed animating a few close-up scenes featuring the pig-like goon. His face was perfect for broad
dialogue shapes and distortions throughout his head.

John's work on one of Maleficent's goons.
© *Disney*

314

The flat graphic styling of Disney characters continued, as the studio began work on *One Hundred and One Dalmatians*. By this time Lounsbery had done enough work applying the new approach to drawing that his animation of Cruella's henchmen Jasper and Horace fit right into the overall look of the film. Live-action reference was filmed for every human character to aid the animators in their animated performances. Yet it is interesting to note that, while Roger and Anita often show traces of live-action in the film, Jasper and Horace's origins seem to be the animator's imagination entirely. This speaks for the way John made use of the live-action reference. He was able to take the actors' ideas for certain scenes, but made considerable changes in order to produce believable drawn personality animation. Lounsbery punched up the timing, he would strengthen the key poses and push the feeling of weight. When Jasper and Horace engage in a conversation with Nanny at the Radcliffs' front door, they pretend to be from the electric company and need access to the home. Their faces are animated with great elasticity as their mood changes from false politeness to sincere annoyance, when Nanny refuses them entry.

Jasper and Horace Badun from One Hundred and One Dalmatians. *© Disney*

MODEL DRG H301

315

John also supervised the animation of the Colonel, a befuddled but likeable English sheepdog, who acts as the self-proclaimed leader of the small group of farm animals, that includes the cat Sergeant Tibs and the horse Captain. The Colonel's eyes are covered by long hair, which presents a challenge to the animator. How can specific expressions be drawn without showing eyes?

John divided the dog's top hair into two parts and animated them as eyebrows. Together with the flexible mouth unit he was able to draw any attitude that was required during his performances.

The Colonel presented the challenge of how to show expression without visible eyes.
© Disney

On the 1963 film *The Sword in the Stone*, Lounsbery again followed Milt Kahl's lead when animating Merlin and Sir Ector. Milt's draftsmanship proved a challenge to match (especially the way he drew hands), and John's graphic version of these characters differ slightly, but the performances are solid and believable. When John had the chance to animate a character without Kahl's input, his animation feels looser and more personal. During the wizards' duel, Madam Mim changes herself into different animals, including a chicken trying to get to Merlin as a worm, and a rhinoceros who overpowers Merlin as a crab. Mim as a chicken is insanely excited because she thinks she has the upper hand, until Merlin as a walrus falls from the sky on top of her. As a rhino she is confident that her heavy weight will smash Merlin, but the magician turns himself into a goat and kicks Mim down a ledge into the water.

Mim as a chicken…
© Disney

…and as a rhino.
© Disney

317

Following *The Sword in the Stone* was *The Jungle Book*, which turned out to be the last animated film Walt Disney supervised. By that time the group of directing animators had shrunk to only four: Milt Kahl, Ollie Johnston, Frank Thomas, and John Lounsbery. Other animators had either left the studio or they functioned in non-supervisory roles. Nevertheless the movie became one of the studio's major hits, particularly in Europe. John got the assignment of animating Colonel Hathi and his herd of elephants. Every character in this film is beautifully developed as a character, and Hathi is no exception. He is a member of Her Majesty's Fifth Pachyderm Brigade, and therefore demands respect and military readiness. Lounsbery was in his element bringing this oversized personality to life. Just the way he walks during the march as well as during inspection has so much character. He is an old-school military type, and even though he is past his prime, military drill still runs through his veins. John made great use of his loose skin around his neck during dialogue scenes. Even his tusks are involved when he talks, and are part of the overall facial squash and stretch. (In theory this goes against rules of anatomy, since an elephant's tusks are connected firmly to his skull, not his flexible jaw.)

The retired Colonel still retains his military bearing.
© *Disney*

To the dismay of his herd, Hathi re-recites the story of when he received a special military award: "It was then I received the Victoria Cross for bravery above and beyond the call of duty. Ha, ha, discipline, discipline was the thing!" His slow walk toward camera during the line is one of the best animated personality locomotions ever. He looks extremely pleased with himself as he rotates a leg outward, before slamming it to the ground, parallel to the opposite leg.

John Lounsbery enjoyed bringing Colonel Hathi's oversized personality to life.
© Disney

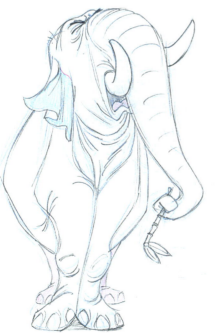
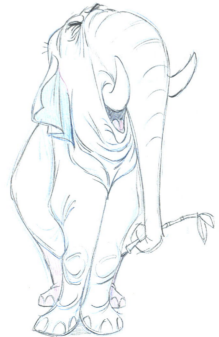
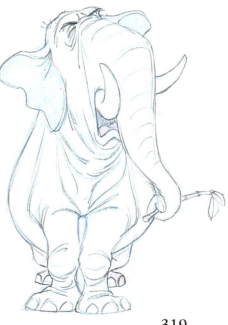

After *The Jungle Book*'s success, the studio continued producing lighthearted ani-mated comedies with productions like *The Aristocats* and *Robin Hood*. Lounsbery was again assigned to animating characters that had been designed and developed by Milt Kahl. He drew scenes with the butler Edgar and the lawyer Georges Hautecourt for *The Aristocats*.

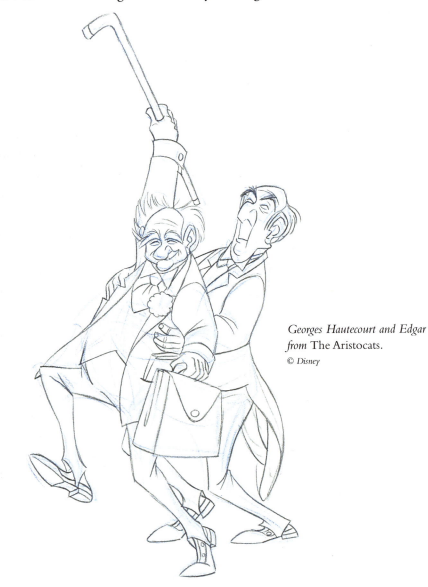

Georges Hautecourt and Edgar from The Aristocats.
© Disney

For *Robin Hood*, John animated scenes that involved the Sheriff of Nottingham and Otto, the hound dog.

The animation on those last assignments is very good, but somehow John felt he was working in the shadow of Milt Kahl, who was still given the opportunity to express his own style when it came to developing new Disney characters. (As Milt put it: "I WAS the Disney style!")

Because John was so well-liked around the studio, and the fact that he enjoyed mentoring young artists led to the decision to make him a co-director on the next film, *The Rescuers*. Lounsbery missed the drawing board though, and had hopes to return to animating in the future. Unfortunately his untimely death prevented this from happening. Today many animation students gravitate toward studying Lounsbery's vast body of work. His comedic acting and his fine drawing abilities combined with his bold use of squash and stretch are worthy of close investigation. John himself would be flattered by all of this attention. He stated modestly toward the end of his life: "I just worked hard and kept trying to become a good animator."

The Sheriff of Nottingham collects tax money from inside Otto's cast.
© *Disney*

321

Pinocchio

1940
HONEST JOHN AND GIDEON
ROUGH ANIMATION
Seq. 3, Sc. 45.2

In most cases two characters who share a scene are drawn on different levels, unless they touch, in which case they are drawn on the same sheet.

Gideon is trying desperately to free Honest John from the awkward predicament he had put the fox in. The scene description in the animation draft reads like this:

EXT. CU – CAT biting fingernails – timidly reaches up – lifts lid of hat – Fox yells: "GET ME OUT OF HERE!" Cat scared, closes lid of hat – pats it – then gets brilliant idea.

This kind of a scene calls for broad staging of the poses as well as crisp timing.

Logic goes out the window when Honest John attempts to remove his hat. There is no way the whole fox head would fit into these squashed drawings, but it looks funny, and that's the important thing.

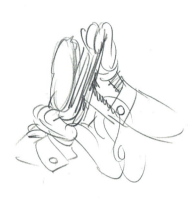

© Disney

322

Lady and the Tramp

1955
JOE
CLEAN-UP ANIMATION
Seq. 7, Sc. 68

Tony, the proprietor of the Italian restaurant, argues with Joe, his chef, who questions his boss' announcement that Tramp just ordered diner. "Tony, dogs don'ta talk!"

In this scene Tony responds vigorously: "He'sa talking to *me*!"

Energetic hand gestures emphasize his attitude, and his expressions are broad and extreme. The body is holding relatively still, so the motion of hands and face reads clearly. Lounsbery was an expert in drawing hands and had no problems depicting them from any angle, as is evident in these key drawings.

There are only two main poses in this scene. During the first one Tony's hands gesture away from his body. The second pose shows him pressing his hands against his chest on the word "*me*." The animation is energetic, but carefully controlled, so it doesn't come off as looking too busy.

© *Disney*

13

19

24

34

37

43

Sleeping Beauty

1959
KING HUBERT
ROUGH ANIMATION
Seq. 13, Sc. 28

"Never underestimate the value of props in animation!" Milt Kahl once said.

John Lounsbery knew this very well, and when he animated this scene, a bottle came in handy to help King Hubert punch a line of dialogue.

Hubert and King Stefan argue over the possibility of their children not liking each other, before they are supposed to get married. Hubert angrily approaches Stefan: "Why doesn't your daughter like my son?" Lounsbery wanted to emphasize the word "son," and there are many ways he could have done this, like banging his fist on the table. But, since earlier on, the two kings were happily toasting and drinking wine, it seems a good choice to use a wine bottle.

Lounsbery feels comfortable portraying strong, exaggerated emotions, and every one of these drawings was done with ease and pleasure.

© Disney

326

The Sword in the Stone

1963
MERLIN
CLEAN-UP ANIMATION
Seq. 2, Sc. 309

Merlin begins to educate Wart about the world as they both leave his house in the woods: "Everybody has problems; the world is full of problems." The magician closes the door behind him, before realizing that his long beard has got stuck. In an effort to free himself, the beard snaps away from the door and ends up in a tight loop around Merlin's neck. He uses his magic wand to uncurl the beard. After three efforts it finally comes loose, but forms a giant, fluffed hairball.

This close up scene shows Merlin's attempts to straighten out his beard to its natural shape. He uses both arms repeatedly to bring it back to its original appearance.

This visual gag helps define Merlin's befuddled charm. He is far from being the perfect, dignified sorcerer. It is interesting to note that the beard takes on a completely abstract shape after being pulled. This transformation comes unexpectedly, and gets a big laugh.

© Disney

17

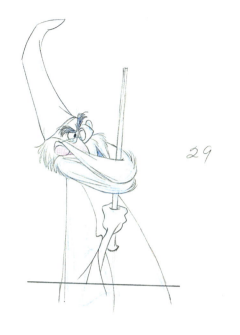

29

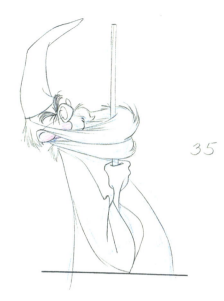

35

59

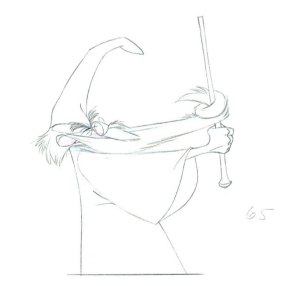

65

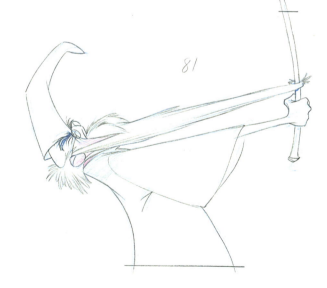

81

329

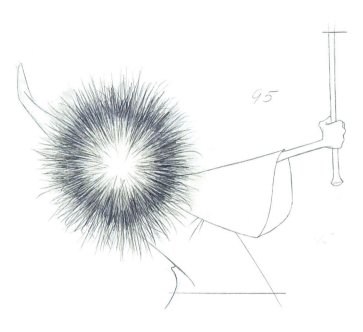

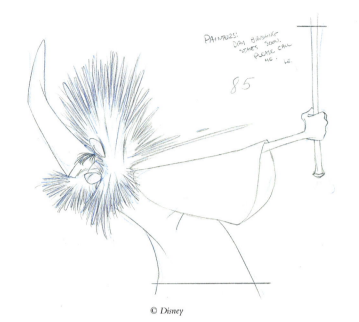

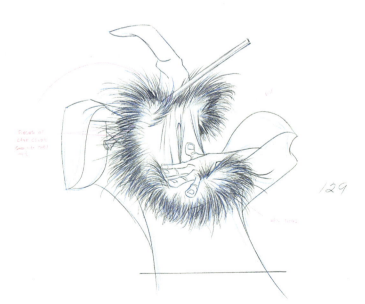

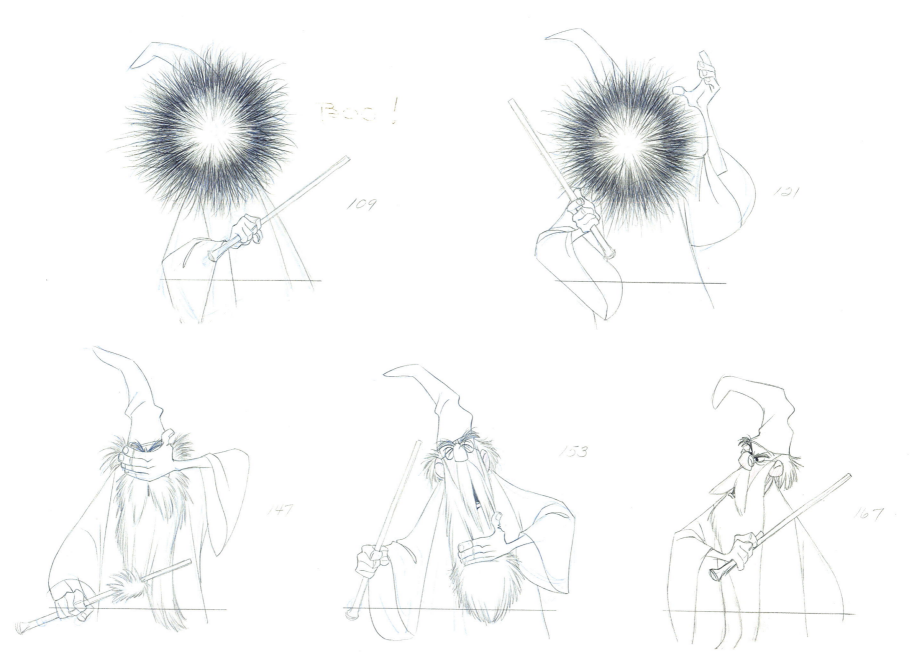

331

The Jungle Book

1967
BALOO AND KING LOUIE
CLEAN-UP ANIMATION
Seq. 7, Sc. 68

During the song "I Wanna Be Like You" Baloo, disguised as an ape, and King Louie end up sharing a few dance moves. As things escalate, Baloo grabs the orangutan from the back and catapults him forward. This is a short continuity scene, but Lounsbery's animation shows careful choreography and drawing during this wild moment.

The reversal of Baloo's spine, when he lifts and throws King Louie, helps to give this action the correct physicality. The scene works without any cartoony distortions, Lounsbery maintains proper anatomy for the two characters throughout. A simple but spirited piece of animation.

© *Disney*

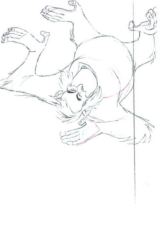

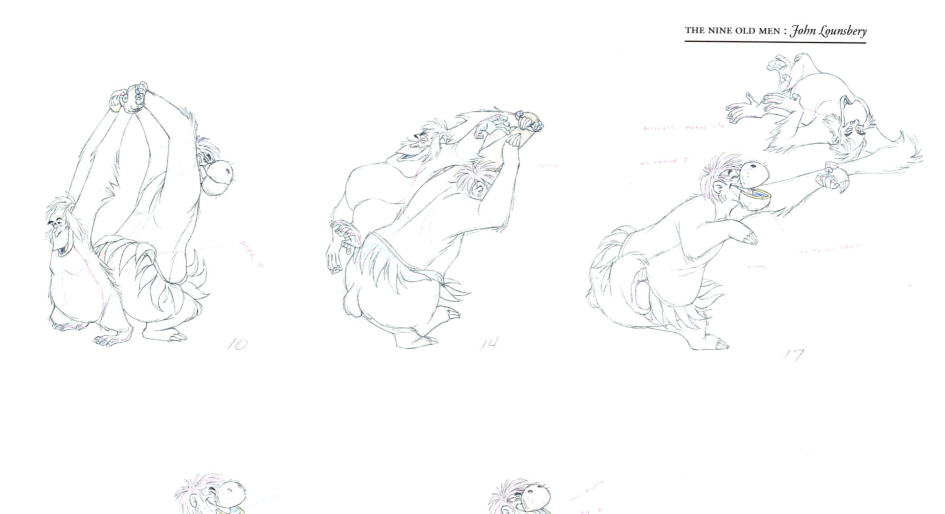

Marc Davis

*A**fter** finishing work on the film *One Hundred and One Dalmatians* in 1960 Marc Davis was looking forward to developing the European tale *Chanticleer* as a possible follow-up animated feature. The story centered on a cocky rooster who believed that he himself was responsible for each sunrise because of his early morning crowing. Marc drew endless designs for this character and the rest of the cast. There were chickens, ducks, foxes, owls, and many other animal types. He also storyboarded several sequences for the project. When the time came to present this work-in-progress to Walt Disney and several businesspeople, Marc was anxious to share what he had been working on. After the designs and story work were pitched, an awkward silence dominated the room. Before Walt could make a comment, one executive bawled: "You can't get a personality out of a chicken!" The group left the office without any further discussion.

Marc was crushed. He felt let down after just having pitched some of the best drawings he ever did at the studio. It tuned out that was the moment his career as an animator was over. Moving forward Marc needed a different kind of artistic challenge, and when Walt Disney offered Marc a top position in his Imagineering department, Marc accepted. This new job still offered the challenge to bring things to life, but not through drawings on film. Instead Walt needed Marc to develop and design electronic mechanisms that would animate robotic figures such as Mr. Lincoln, children from around the world, and a great number of pirates. Disney animation lost one of its all-time greats, but Disneyland benefited greatly from Marc's artistic influence on some of the most iconic theme park rides. His 25 years as an animator and story-man provided the perfect experience for telling stories within a real environment inhabited by all sorts of Audio-Animatronics characters.

Back in 1935, young Marc Davis was looking for a job as a newspaper cartoonist, but this was the time of the Great Depression and steady employment was hard to find. One day he found out that Walt Disney was looking for artists to help him expand the art of animation. He applied and was hired on the spot. His portfolio was full of thorough human and animal anatomical studies.

They showed a standard and level of draftsmanship never before seen in an applicant's submission. Marc had spent years drawing animals at the San Francisco Zoo, where he observed their skeletal structure but also their individual ways of moving. With no prior animation background, he received training to become an assistant animator. When the studio began animation for *Snow White and the Seven Dwarfs*, Marc was asked by senior animator Grim Natwick to assist him on the character of Snow White herself. Natwick's drawing style was loose and sketchy, but he knew that a fine draftsman like Davis would be a great asset to him for maintaining the realistic look of the princess. Marc at first was a little surprised to be asked to draw the girl; after all, he had been known around the studio for being an expert in depicting animals. But the way he sketched the female form in life drawing classes was equally impressive. As a matter of fact, this early assignment would be the start of his career as an animator of leading ladies, both good and evil.

Natwick was grateful for Marc's fine work on the title character, and he offered him the chance to animate a couple of scenes during the dance sequence with the dwarfs. Marc knew that drawing Snow White's head looking good at any angle would not be an easy task to accomplish. So he produced a small sculpture of her head that would help him define correct facial perspectives. Looking at his first animation, it is astonishing to see how elegantly Snow White moves as she dances in the dwarfs' cottage. The main motion was based on live-action reference, but the overlapping action of her hair and dress needed to be enhanced and broadened in order to look natural in animation.

*Snow White dances
in the dwarfs' cottage.*
© *Disney*

337

She certainly wasn't an easy character to get started on as an animator and learn the tricks of the trade, because everything about Snow White is subtle. Usually newcomers to the animated medium receive assignments with broad characters like Goofy or Donald Duck, who require a much more extensive use of squash and stretch in the animation. Marc wouldn't get the chance to work on such types until years later. His last assistant work was for the 1938 short film *Ferdinand the Bull*, before Walt Disney asked Marc to join the story unit for *Bambi*, a film he would work on for the next six years. Everyone at the studio knew about Marc's expertise in animal drawing, and since the film's characters were to be drawn with more realism than ever before, only top draftsmen were assigned to the movie. At the beginning, Marc needed to figure out an appropriate design style for Bambi, Thumper, Flower, and the rest of the cast.

These personalities were supposed to express human emotions while retaining their specific animal behavior. If drawn too realistically, they would not be much fun to animate. If drawn in a very caricatured way, they would not match the serious tone of the story material.

Luckily even as a young artist Marc had good judgment and his early drawings show just the right combination of real animal anatomy and animatable forms. In order to give young Bambi childlike expressions, Marc studied photographs from a book about juvenile behavior. The results impressed Walt Disney and animator Frank Thomas, who later stated: "Without all of Marc's design research, we couldn't have made the movie."

FACING PAGE
These head studies show that Bambi was able to go through a wide range of human emotions.
© Disney

1-002 © W.D.P.

BAMBI BABY
EXPRESSIONS

SHEET #41 — OCT. 21, 1939

Marc spent four years developing story sequences that would inspire background artists and animators to bring the world of *Bambi* to life. The extraordinary draftsmanship in these sketches proved that there was great potential in translating Felix Salten's book into an animated feature film. The poses are solid, and their staging makes the characters relate strongly.

These sketches show Davis' extraordinary draftsmanship.
© Disney

Toward the end of story development on *Bambi*, Walt Disney told Marc that he would like to see his drawings on the screen, but animated. "So he sent me to see Frank Thomas and Milt Kahl. Walt asked them to make an animator out of me," Marc recounted later. A short training period followed, during which Marc studied the work methods and philosophies of these two established animators. Milt Kahl brought superior drawing and grand design to his scenes, while Frank Thomas always started out by analyzing the character's emotions. Eventually Marc was assigned to the character of Flower, a kind and melancholic skunk. A de-scented live animal was brought to the studio, providing Marc with the opportunity to study his subject up close. Before animating his first scene, he created many rough model studies of real skunks in order to achieve the realism needed for the final version.

Early studies show Marc's attempts to capture the essence of a skunk. Black and white fur markings already create interesting design patterns.
© *Disney*

1-002
SKUNK LIFE SKETCHES
Sheet #21 12/10/38

341

Further explorations lead to the final character design, but even at this stage it was important to Marc to develop a full understanding of the inner structure of this cartoon animal.

Once the inner workings of the skunk's body are explored, the animation will appear believable and plausible.
© Disney

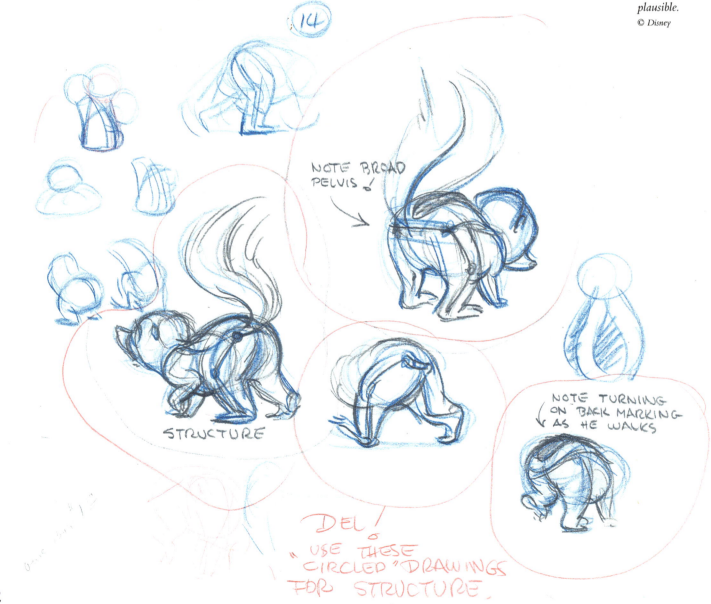

Marc ended up drawing most of Flower's scenes as well as the ones that involved a girl skunk. When these two characters meet, they are instantly twitterpated, and the situation turns into the most surreal and cartoony sequence of the whole film. After a few flirtatious gestures their mouths "accidentally" make contact, resulting in a surprise kiss. Flower actually blushes, he turns bright pink, and his body takes on the shape of a square brick. He then falls backward and bounces on the ground like a stiff piece of wood. It is a very unusual gag within this realistic film. Audiences were used to watching Donald or Goofy going through routines like this one, but to see Flower's reaction of his first kiss being portrayed in such a broad manner must have seemed somewhat unexpected. The reason the scene works and always gets a big laugh is because Marc had previously established Flower as a completely convincing character in the way he moved and expressed himself. His soft-spoken voice suggested slow and subtle movements. But here, by contrast, his feelings of first love turn into an over-the-top animated moment. Through it, the skunk becomes even more likeable because he shows that even he is capable of an extreme emotion such as love and passion.

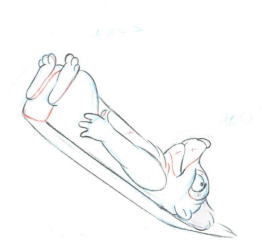

Flower's over-the-top reaction to his first kiss was unusual in the otherwise realistic film, but Marc Davis made it work.
© Disney

Intense emotions were again called for when Marc Davis briefly returned to story work for the wartime propaganda documentary *Victory Through Air Power*. The film was based on the book by Major Alexander de Seversky. Marc developed the final climactic battle between the American Eagle and the Japanese Octopus. This is a short sequence, but highly dramatic staging and editing combined with a stylized color palette created dramatic moments.

It is interesting to point out that Marc's story sketches made it virtually unchanged to the screen.

All the power and drama evident in his drawings was captured by the sequence's art direction and Bill Tytla's powerful animation.

These story sketches show Davis' ability to visualize a fierce action sequence.
© Disney

345

By the early 1940s, Walt Disney was aware of Marc's multiple talents as an animator, story-man, and designer. The film *Song of the South* was in early development, and Marc was the first animator to be assigned to the project. He started out by exploring a style for the animal characters. Even in these initial sketches, Marc is already looking for ways to enhance the personalities graphically. While these character types walk on two legs, they retain their distinctive animal attributes: the cunning fox and the slow but strong bear.

The personalities of Brer Fox and Brer Bear (opposite) come across even in these early sketches.
© *Disney*

346

In this film, Marc animated the introductory scene with Brer Rabbit when he is telling Uncle Remus that he decided to run away from his home in the Briar Patch. In the process of nailing his front door shut with a hammer, he hits one of his fingers. Things get worse when he angrily hits the hammer with one leg, which causes great pain and leads him to take a few jumps as he holds on to his foot. All the way through the scene he is carrying on a conversation with Uncle Remus about all the trouble he is getting into. It's a terrific piece of acting business and reveals Brer Rabbit as a somewhat nervous and energetic, yet likeable character.

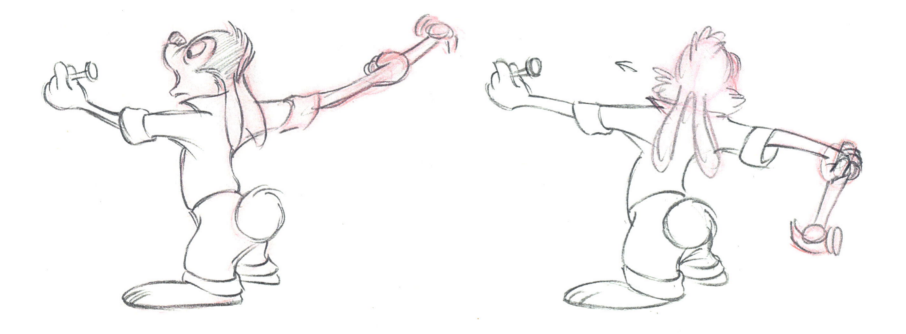

*Right from the first scene Marc lets the audience
know what kind of character Brer Rabbit is.*
© Disney

349

GESTIONS
DRESS ANIMALS BUILD
6/2/48
PROD. 1020

After completing animation on several key scenes with each of the three main characters Marc went on to work on movies like *Fun and Fancy Free* and *The Adventures of Ichabod and Mr. Toad*, but not in an animation supervisory role. It just so happened that by the time he was assigned to any of these films, the top spots had already been filled by other animators. Frustrating as this might have been, Marc still produced solid character animation for the *Bongo* section as well as the *Mr. Toad* sequence. When *Cinderella* went into production, Marc did again join the group of directing animators. He helped design the title character's appearance as well as some of her outfits.

Cinderella's charming but mild-mannered demeanor presented a challenge for Marc Davis and Eric Larson, who supervised her animation. A character who doesn't show strong emotions is very difficult to bring to life. Without any eccentricities to play with, your range as an animator is somewhat limited. Only subtle and realistic motion is called for. And yet there are moments in the film when Cinderella projects feelings such as anger and even cynicism.

When the stepmother is holding a music lesson for her two rather untalented daughters, Cinderella is cleaning the floor downstairs while singing her song "Sing Sweet Nightingale." All of a sudden she realizes that Lucifer, the cat, has left dirty footprints all over the floor. Cinderella angrily tosses the washing cloth and goes after the evil cat, when suddenly there is a knock at the front door. She opens it and receives a letter from the palace. The mice witnessing the situation are as surprised as she is. Cinderella wonders about the letter's content, then turns to the mice and says: "Maybe I should interrupt the 'music lesson?'" Her brief, wide-eyed expression clearly communicates what she really thinks about the singing coming from upstairs. This scene along with many others was acted out by actress Helene Stanley. Her filmed performances served as a basis for the animators' work. Marc knew exactly how to work with such reference; he chose carefully which parts of the live-action were important to his animated performance and which parts proved extraneous.

*Cinderella and the
letter from the palace.*
© *Disney*

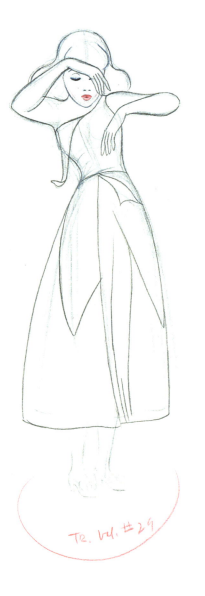

Marc also animated the iconic moment when Cinderella's ragged outfit—with the help of the Fairy Godmother—is transformed into a beautiful gown. It is common knowledge that this scene became a favorite of Walt Disney. Marc stated later rather modestly: "It's not because of my animation. This scene represents Walt's philosophy that good things can happen, that your dreams can come true."

It is interesting to see that the final clean-up drawings were made right over Marc's rough animation drawings. This process saved time, but was only possible whenever the animator drew the character completely on model.
© Disney

The animation of Cinderella required top-notch draftsmanship, and Walt knew that the heroine for his next feature *Alice in Wonderland* also needed to be assigned to animators who were competent in animating a female lead. It is obvious why Marc ended up in the unit that was responsible for bringing Alice to life. He did not necessary welcome the assignment, because he knew that the film's entertainment would come from all of its eccentric characters, such as the Mad Hatter or the Queen of Hearts. While personalities like Cinderella or Alice don't make audiences laugh out loud, they are essential to the story and must be handled in a believable way—they need to come across as real. When watching *Alice in Wonderland*, the audience takes on the role of Alice, who reacts constantly to the nonsensical characters and situations she finds herself in.

Marc animated her in the Mad Tea Party sequence as she tries to solve silly riddles and plays along during a manic unbirthday party. Based on live-action reference Marc produced the most appealing and delicate drawings of Alice. Each of his rough animation drawings is so carefully executed that they hold up as individual illustrations. They are a joy to look at for more than a twenty-fourth of a second.

Marc's rough drawings are delicate and appealing.
© *Disney*

The animator explores the dimensional forms of Alice's face in detail.
© *Disney*

353

Marc's next assignment would be a female character again, but this time her personality was capable of a wider range of emotions. Tinker Bell from the film *Peter Pan* did not talk, which presented an interesting challenge to the animator. Her whole body language needed to communicate her inner feelings, which were mostly driven by her jealousy toward Wendy. And even though Tinker Bell at one point puts Wendy's life in danger, Marc manages to present her as an utterly likable character. We see her first in the Darling children's bedroom as she lands on a mirror to inspect her reflection. Her mood changes from delight to shock when Tink notices the size of her hips. This reaction makes her instantly relatable and sympathetic.

Designed with ultimate appeal and feminine elegance, Tinker Bell admires her mirror image.
© Disney

Marc's animation sketches were turned into clean-up drawings by Clair Weeks.
© Disney

When Peter Pan's first attempts to teach the children how to fly fail, Tinker Bell is delighted. Wendy, John, and Michael fall from the room's ceiling and crash on to a bed. Tink observes the situation sitting on an alphabet cube. She laughs mischievously, which causes the cube to turn over, resulting in her own crash—a lesson about the fact that taking pleasure in the misfortunes of others will often have consequences! Clean-up artist Clair Weeks turned Marc's animation sketches for this scene into delicate clean-up drawings while maintaining a very high level of draftsmanship.

One of Marc's "doodle" sheets shows his research for Tinker Bell's facial features and hair movement. By placing her mouth low and practically eliminating the jaw, she appears more pixie-like and less realistic.
© *Disney*

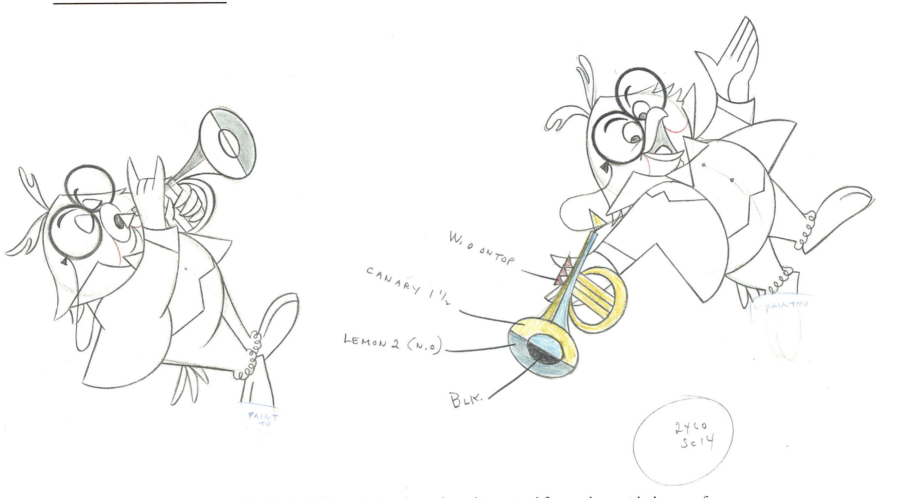

CANARY 1 1/2

W, 0 ON TOP

LEMON 2 (N.0)

BLK.

PAINT TO

PAINT TO

2460
SC 14

While Tinker Bell was designed as a three-dimensional figure, along with the rest of the cast of *Peter Pan*, graphic changes were starting to surface at The Walt Disney Studio during the 1950s.

Marc Davis was one of a few artists who influenced this development, while other animators initially resented the modern two-dimensional approach to drawing. Pablo Picasso had become the world's most celebrated artist, and Marc—together with Milt Kahl and Ward Kimball—welcomed a change in character styling influenced by modern art. In 1953, Kimball directed the short film *Toot, Whistle, Plunk and Boom*, which turned

*Strong curved and straight lines define
the appearance of the film's characters.*
© *Disney*

out to be a clever history lesson about musical instruments. Its character designs resemble flat paper cut-outs, imagery found in mid-century cubist art. Marc Davis was one of the key animators who worked on the short, and he welcomed the challenge of animating within this new graphic, sophisticated style. The characters of course still needed to act and entertain, but the way they were drawn indicated that a new era had begun at Walt's studio. For this groundbreaking film, Marc focused on developing the outgoing personality of the narrator, Professor Owl.

357

This change in approach to drawing continued on and was further developed for Disney's elaborate feature *Sleeping Beauty*. Marc skipped the production of *Lady and the Tramp*, allowing him to design, animate, and establish *Sleeping Beauty's* two main characters, Aurora and Maleficent. During a lecture Marc explained: "We did a lot more design with the characters than we had ever done before or would ever do again. Sleeping Beauty was more designed in two-dimensional shapes than any other character we've done."

This initial design represents a young, princess, who does look 16 years old.
© Disney

MARC DAVIS

In the final version, Aurora's age could be 25. It is unclear why this aging process took place, perhaps a juvenile-looking girl didn't fit the film's sophisticated story.
© Disney

*In this elegant key drawing, Aurora dances with a prince
made up of various animals, including an owl and a squirrel.
What a beautiful composition, even for a back view!*
© *Disney*

Because
of the degree of
realism in the character's
design, actress Helene Stanley
was again called upon to act out most
scenes for Marc Davis as reference for his animation. He later explained to students about his use of
live action. Marc compared this footage to a first rough pass of
a scene: "You don't start from scratch with a blank piece of paper, you
already have something to look at." The idea is to take what an actor has done
and translate it into graphic, moving statements. Simply tracing the photostats would
result in "floaty" animation without enough contrast in the timing. While some parts of
a scene need to be sped up, others might have to be slowed down in order to feel right for
graphic motion. Then there are special design patterns in Aurora's hair and the fabric of her
skirt. These things need to be invented and controlled by the animator. When the overall
live acting is not satisfactory, the scene has to be reimagined by way of conventional animation. It's fair to say that using live-action reference successfully is not as easy as it might
seem. Marc animated Aurora's most important acting scenes, including her encounter with
the sympathetic forest animals, who desperately want the girl to find her prince.

359

The film's villainess offered even greater and more dramatic design possibilities. Maleficent needed to look visually stunning as well as intimidating. Her personality and voice were dominant and authoritative, and Marc new how to match those qualities with pencil and paper.

An early version of Maleficent's design.
© *Disney*

360

In the end, added horns gave her appearance
a devilish quality, and sleeves shaped like
flames were used to great dramatic effect.
© Disney

361

Marc took great pleasure in drawing this theatrical-looking character, but bringing her to life through animation was a different matter. As he stated, Maleficent for most of the time stood around giving speeches. She never came in physical contact with any of the other characters. This presented limitations in what you can do with her. Subdued acting and slow carefully conceived movements helped to make her believable to an audience.

The raven added a nice visual touch, and he also gave Maleficent the opportunity for some acting business. She could stroke his feathers or put him on her shoulder. The raven was also important as a story device when he is being sent away to look far and wide for the whereabouts of the princess.

A couple of dynamic, rough sketches demonstrate the way Marc lays out key moments of a scene, before animating it.
© *Disney*

363

After spending close to five years working on *Sleeping Beauty*, where each drawing reached a level of perfection never attempted before, Marc received what would become the ultimate assignment of his animation career. Cruella De Vil in *One Hundred and One Dalmatians* encompasses all the qualities we have come to love in a Disney villain. Her over-the-top design is a graphic masterpiece, her ambitions are truly evil, and her bombastic screen presence makes her a favorite among animation fans. Unlike Maleficent, Cruella is very physical in her actions. She slaps her henchmen Jasper and Horace, she threatens Anita and Roger by getting up close to them, and she drives her car into a snowdrift while pursuing the dogs. Her drawing is full of contrast: a tall skinny body with extremely thin arms and legs, covered by an enormous fur coat. With that kind of dramatic portrayal, it is no surprise that she steals every scene she is in.

What is surprising is the fact that Marc Davis animated every single scene with this character.

Yet Cruella is not a simple design to draw. There are multiple sections of her fur coat, and just her handbag alone is very detailed. Marc animated her often on ones, which requires 24 drawings per second (animation on twos uses only 12). All this meant extra work, more working hours, and endless dedication. Cruella went through many design explorations before Marc found his villainess. All sorts of hairstyles, fur coat designs, and different facial features were considered at one time or another.

Actress Mary Wickes was filmed as she acted out many of Cruella's scenes, but Marc's animation goes so much further than Wickes' performances. He exaggerated each gesture to maximize her flamboyancy. The fur coat's motion re-enforces Cruella's broad action, as it swings back and forth before coming to a stop. In order to make the coat feel heavy, it needed to be timed carefully. Anything heavy takes longer to change direction than something light, like a thin skirt.

For most scenes, Marc did every other drawing, with one even in-between left for the assistant to do. Most other animators would often call for two or three in-betweens to be done.

FACING PAGE
Early ideas for Cruella De Vil's design.
© *Disney*

But Marc's philosophy was that the more drawings he did for a given scene, the more he controlled the action. Cruella De Vil became one of the most entertaining screen creations ever.

As an audience we can't take our eyes off her because everything she does is shocking, surprising, or hilarious. If an animator ever left the medium on a high note it is Marc Davis with his unforgettable creation of Cruella De Vil.

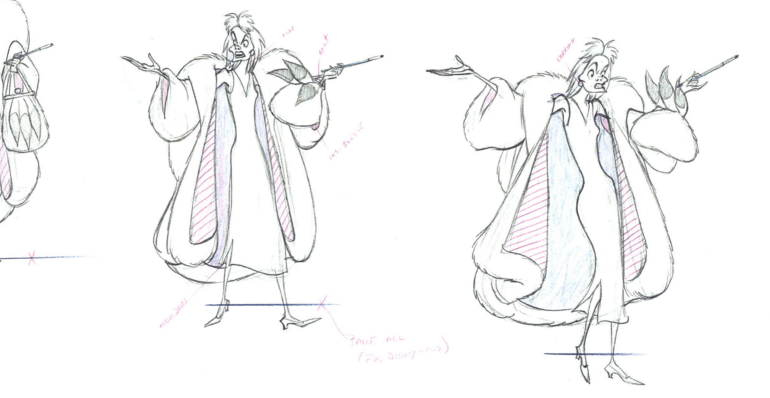

We can't help but wonder what artistic influence Marc might have had on future films like *The Jungle Book* or *Robin Hood*, but we will never know. Walt Disney needed him in other areas of his organization. Marc's unique body of animated work set such a high standard that studying it can be somewhat intimidating. His characters are masterfully drawn and they show a huge range in their performances. Marc was able to capture the innocence of Flower, the skunk, as well as dramatic, theatrical qualities for characters like Maleficent and Cruella. But he would not want his work to intimidate; instead he would want it to inspire future generations of animators.

Cruella De Vil is one of the most entertaining screen creations ever.
© *Disney*

Bambi

1942
FLOWER AND THUMPER
CLEAN-UP ANIMATION
Seq. 10.1, Sc. 41

When adult Bambi, Flower, and Thumper run into friend Owl, they are being warned of becoming "twitterpated": "...you run smack into a pretty face. Woo-woo!"

In this scene Marc animated Flower being spooked, as he jumps into the arms of Thumper, looking for protection. Thumper is not pleased and pushes the skunk off.

This is a cartoony moment, but the animation comes off as very believable, because both characters move with weight. As soon as Flower makes contact with Thumper, both characters swing to one side, before they settle back into a pose. The audience will believe in impossible situations as long as the animation shows real weight.

© Disney

368

TR#1A FOOT

9

TR#1A FOOT

17

FOOT TRIBAL#1A

23

TRIBAL#1A

40

TRIBAL#1A

TRIBAL FOOT#53A

43

TRIBAL FOOT#1A

FOOT TRIBAL #53A

46

*C*inderella

1950
CINDERELLA
CLEAN-UP ANIMATION
Seq. 3, Sc. 10

The Fairy Godmother tells Cinderella: "You can't go to the ball looking like that."

Her melancholic reaction is subtle and underplayed: "The ball? But I'm not…"

Marc knew that simplicity is best when showing a character feeling dejected.

Cinderella lowers her head as she glances at her torn dress. Her hands hold it up slightly as a sort of reality check. The ball is out of reach now.

When a realistic character like Cinderella moves in such an understated way, the quality of the drawing becomes paramount. In particular, her face needs to be drawn with perfection from any angle. Cinderella's expression is a mixture of resignation, but also dignity. The audience feels a certain pathos and clearly roots for the girl.

370

© Disney

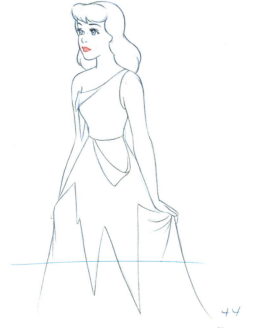

Sleeping Beauty

1959
AURORA
ROUGH ANIMATION
Seq. 12, Sc.17

"Everything is so wonderful, just wait 'til you meet him!" Aurora tells the three good fairies that she is in love, and what better way to express her emotions than twirling around in dance-like fashion? Marc made use of two elements that help the animation appear graceful and fluid. Aurora's long, curly hair is beautifully designed as it flares out during the turn around. The same can be said for the many lines defining folds on her skirt. It is interesting to note that as the character directs her attention from screen left to right, her upper body is leading the motion. The lower body moves slightly in the opposite direction for balance. Even during her acting scenes, Marc always maintained an element of elegance and fluency.

© Disney

372

53

57

65

89

93

Sleeping Beauty

1959
MALEFICENT
ROUGH ANIMATION
Seq. 18, Sc. 67

Maleficent leaves the dungeon, in which Prince Phillip is being held captive. She locks the door with a key and puts it into her pocket. "For the first time in 16 years I shall sleep well," she tells her raven. This is a sequence of stunning drawings reminiscent of elegant fashion illustrations. The main motion here is the key traveling from the door lock into Maleficent's pocket. The audience follows this move very clearly since her overall action is very slight and gradual.

In scenes like this one, it must have been a challenge to keep the raven firmly placed on Maleficent's shoulder, since her oversized collar could get in the way.

But, Marc always manages to stage the raven convincingly with the collar either in front or behind him.

49

© Disney

57

376

© Disney

137

153

*O*ne *H*undred and *O*ne *D*almatians

1961
CRUELLA DE VIL
TOUCH-UP ANIMATION
Seq. 16, Sc. 182

Cruella gets her comeuppance in her final scene of the film. In trying to push over the truck in which the Dalmatians are hiding, her car collides with Jasper and Horace's vehicle. All three end up down an embankment among car wreckage. "You idiots! You...you fools! Oh, you imbeciles...ah, ha, ha..." Jasper responds: "Aw, shut up!"

Marc was able to turn Cruella's desperate finale into a highly entertaining scene.

He drew her looking exasperated and disheveled. Yet ultimately there is something hilarious about the way her torn fur coat barely hangs on to her body. Every frustrated move she makes is being enhanced by the follow-through action of her lower coat.

The scene might have been Marc's final piece of animation, and it is a masterpiece. Drawing and motion look grotesque and bizarre, but appealing at the same time.

© Disney

380

Animator: An artist who brings characters to life (in regards to this book, the artist's technique is the use of pencil and paper).

Background: A painting that serves as the backdrop and stage for the animated character.

Cartoony: The term for describing an animation style that is broad and exaggerated.

Cel: A transparent sheet of celluloid on which an animation drawing is inked and painted.

Clean-up: The process of refining the lines of rough animation by redrawing a scene in a detailed fine line.

Effects animation: The art of moving special illusions like clouds, water, or shadows in support of the character's actions.

Exposure sheet: A form that details the action, dialogue, and music for a scene. Each horizontal line represents one frame of film.

Extreme drawing: The farthest point of an action or expression.

Flipping: To hold a group of drawings so that they will fall in an even pattern and give the viewer the illusion of movement.

Frame: The individual picture on the film. There are 16 frames to each foot of film, 24 frames to each second of running time on the screen.

Full animation: The process of creating fluid movement by showing between 12 and 24 drawings for each second of film.

Hold: To keep a drawing stationary for a number of frames.

In-betweener: The artist who finishes the needed number of drawings in between those created by the animator. This process is required for rough as well as clean-up animation.

Inker: The artist who traces drawings onto cells with ink.

Layout: The black-and-white rendering done by a layout artist that determines the basic composition of a scene.

Limited animation: The process of using animation drawings economically by often holding the character's pose still and only show mouth movement.

Painter: The artist who paints colors on cells.

Rotoscope: The use of live-action film reference to aid the animator with realistic movements.

Rough: The animator's sketchy drawings.

Squash and stretch: An animation principle that depicts the character in a compressed and elongated position, adding fluidity and comedy to the motion.

Staging: The basic visual presentation of a scene.

Storyboard: A large board on which pinned sketches tell a story in comic-strip fashion.

Story reel: A filmed sequence as a work in progress.

Story sketch: A simple, storytelling drawing done by a story artist.

Sweat box: A small projection room in which films are run for criticism.

Touch-up: The process of tying down the animator's rough drawing on the same sheet of paper by erasing extraneous pencil lines.

385

INDEX

{ Page numbers in italics refer to illustrations }

387

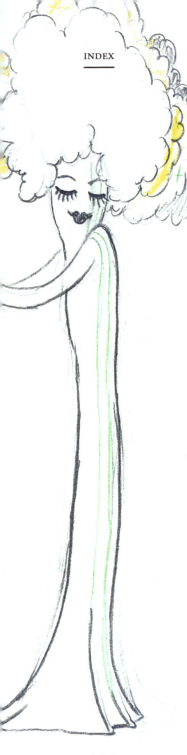

The End